The Alcohol Con

Michaela Weaver

Published by Parker Press Publishing, 2020.

The purpose of this book is to educate, entertain and provide information on the subject matter covered. All attempts have been made to verify information at the time of this publication and the author does not assume responsibility for errors, omissions, or other interpretations of the subject matter. Medical and scientific knowledge is constantly changing, and many factors determine how it is applied in different circumstances. The purchaser or reader should always seek the individualised advice of a medical professional, and this book should not be used as an alternative to such advice which should precede any action being taken. The purchaser or reader of this book assumes responsibility for the use of this material and information. The author assumes to responsibility or liability on behalf of any purchaser of reader of this book.

Edited by Rebecca Martin

Illustrated by Holly Weaver

ISBN: 978-1-912008-70-4

For my dad,

Peter Ward

Always honest, always true and, above all, very
smart!

Contents

x

Introduction

THIRTY YEARS AFTER joining the merry-go-round of drinking alcohol, my thumping head, nauseous stomach, and I, finally saw it for what it was: the biggest con trick on the planet. At that point I metaphorically got off the ride, left the fairground, and walked off into a beautiful sunny day. I'm still walking around in that beautiful sunny world, where it's calm and peaceful, and the war of wants, and shouldn't haves, and hungover regrets has stopped raging in my head.

I don't head for the fridge as soon as I get home from work anymore, and don't curse when I find only a half a bottle left there from the night before. I don't worry about going out with friends and needing to remember to stop drinking after four drinks, only to have four drinks and forget to remember. I don't ever wake up at 3am with a dry throat, and racing heart with a feeling of dread as I try to remember what I said and did the night before. I don't have to deal with my guilt, or feeling stupid because I decided not to have a drink last night, but come wine o'clock my body went into autopilot as my brain decided to change its mind, and I did the very thing I promised myself that I wouldn't do.

I don't do any of that any more because I outsmarted the con artist that had held my confidence and trust for all those years. I outsmarted alcohol, and you can too. Alcohol has no control over me, as I now realise it once did. I am in complete control of every drop of alcohol that passes my lips. I consume exactly the amount of alcohol that I want to drink, which is exactly none.

You can get smart about alcohol, and you can get control over it. But before you can outsmart anything, you need to understand it. In the game of psychological warfare, knowledge is ammunition, and knowledge is power.

But wait a minute.

Surely, if there's a problem with alcohol, then it's the people who drink too much of it that have a problem. After all, isn't the term 'alcohol abuse' aimed at the uncontrolled drinker and not the drink itself.

We all know that it's alcoholics on park benches drinking meths from bottles in paper bags who have a problem. We know it's them who need to go to weekly AA meetings and sit in a circle proclaiming their acquiescence to a lifelong disease and affliction that they battle in misery to control because they were born with some dodgy genes.

We know that we're different and our kind of drinking belongs in a different world. Ours is a world of grown-up laughs, sophisticated choices, and wine o'clock normality.

We've all grown up knowing that drinking alcohol is the golden ticket to adulthood and more alluring than a first kiss. We spent the early years of drinking, proving we could drink like fishes, building up tolerance, and working hard for the badge of being a proper grown up alcohol drinker.

We learned that drinking is the multi-tasking doer of all things: it relaxes, relieves boredom, gives a whoop of joy, helps get over an argument, deals with our stress, fills our hours, brings us our friends, make social occasions fabulous, helps us throw off our clothes in the bedroom, makes us happy, makes us interesting, and the life and soul of the party.

We know all these things. Or we think we do. So why on earth would we need to outsmart it, when it does so much for us, our family, our friends, and everyone we know?

Because if it really did all those things, and there were no consequences, then it would be awesome, it really would. The problem is, as we all know, that if anything seems too good to be true, then it usually is. And alcohol is no exception. Yet virtually every drinker genuinely believes in a long list of benefits that alcohol brings them.

Since birth, we've been conditioned by society, media, and the people we know and love, to believe that drinking alcohol is not only normal, but expected. It is the only drug on the planet that you have to justify not taking. Because alcohol is a drug, although the fact is not widely advertised: you don't see advertisements saying, 'Drink Sauvignon Blanc this Christmas, it's a highly addictive and poisonous drug.'

In terms of addictive power, alcohol sits beside heroin, cocaine and nicotine. It is second to heroin in the addictive stakes, scoring 2.2/3 where heroin scores 2.5/3.

In a UK study by David Nutt of Imperial College London in 2010, alcohol was found to be the most harmful drug on the planet based on 16 criteria relating to harm to the individual and harm to others. In the study, alcohol scored 72/100 compared to the second most dangerous drug, heroin, scoring 55/100, and crack cocaine which scored 54/100. Alcohol is not only harmful to us physically, it harms us psychologically, and it harms our families. Alcohol hurts the people we love.

Alcohol may be harmful, but we all know that in small doses it's good for us. We've been told that it's good for our heart to have a glass of red wine each day. Sadly, as medical knowledge expands, this is another bubble in the alcohol con to burst. The good stuff in red wine is resveratrol, which you can find in strawberries, grapes and blueberries to name a few sources, and these don't come with increased risk of cancer to the neck, head, breast, colon, oesophagus or liver.

A study published in *The Lancet* in 2018 concluded that the level of alcohol consumption per week that minimises health loss is zero. Put another way, this means that for us mere mortals, the safe amount of alcohol to consume is none. The study used 650 data sources, and over 590 studies in reaching its conclusion. Alcohol consumption has now been linked to 60 acute and chronic diseases, and just one glass of wine per day has been linked to a 15% increased risk of breast cancer.

We may know that something is bad for us, but our minds have an amazing ability to convince us that inconvenient facts which stand in the way of us doing what we want to do don't apply to us. The mild inconvenience of the negatives pale into insignificance compared to the enormous benefits that we're convinced that we're getting.

And then one day something changes. Some crisis occurs that affects us personally, and we decide that we have to do something different.

Right now, you probably believe that alcohol is an important part of your life. But you'll also know that supping those glasses of wine or beer each night, or partying hard at the weekend, is causing a problem. Alcohol may be affecting your health, your work, or your relationship, or maybe all three.

You may be realising that the hangovers are feeling worse, or that you feel tired all day until a drink in the evening miraculously wakes you up.

Waking up full of remorse and anxiety, with a thumping head, and a questionable or even non-existent recollection of last night's events is far from fun, relaxing or stress-free. In fact, it's diametrically opposite. And vowing never to do it again only to pour a glass of red wine at dinner isn't good for long term self-esteem, either, as you find yourself in a constant cycle of internal mental battles, over which reaching for a glass always wins.

The result is that the real you, the conscious-minded part of you that doesn't want to drink, fails. Always. And I know, because I always failed too. If I'd had a particularly boozy Saturday night with friends and felt hellish the next day, I'd be proud of myself that I didn't have a glass of wine that evening. The fact that I was still feeling queasy from the night before didn't enter my head as being the reason for my evening of abstinence.

When I decided to stop drinking for a while, like on a hungover 1st of January having decided to do a dry month, I'd start off feeling amazingly positive and determined. All my resolve and positive vision of self, drinking green tea every evening, was primed and ready for action. I would spring open the fridge and give the bottle of wine a 'Ya boo,' scoff before putting it firmly in the back of the cupboard, with a 'See you in February,' smile.

I'd go to the pub and loudly order a diet coke, telling the bar tender that I was doing *Dry January*. I might as well have stood on the bar, grabbed a microphone, and shouted to the room, 'Look at me with my diet coke everyone! Look at me controlling alcohol. I'm not drinking Chardonnay or Merlot here today my friends, so I DON'T HAVE AN ALCOHOL PROBLEM.' Thou doth protest too much.

By around the 20th of January I was usually bored with *Dry January* and poured myself a large chilled glass of white wine to celebrate my abstinence. A week later and I had my nose back in the fridge at wine o'clock, waking up on Saturday morning with a remorseful hangover.

For someone who is fundamentally a smart person, none of that made me feel very smart. And that's the problem, drink makes a fool of everyone, even the most successful and well educated of us.

What you're about to find out is that the whole package that is wrapped up in the glass in your hand is the result of a very clever and long drawn out confidence trick. It's a confidence trick that has drawn you in, like it did me, and millions of others, and one that you have completely trusted.

All con tricks work because the con artist gains your trust, implicitly. You believe in them, who they say they are, and the benefits that you believe they can bring you.

The psychological brainwashing of addiction happens in the subconscious mind, and this is the part of your mind that says, 'Oh go on then,' when your conscious mind is sitting there with its arms crossed and a large banner with the words, 'I'm not going to drink today' emblazoned in bold lettering. This explains why we feel stupid when we've gone to such lengths, just to cave in five minutes later.

If you knew for a fact that you had been a victim of a con trick that had trapped you, would you want to get out?

Alcohol is the basis of a confidence trick of pandemic proportions, with millions of people across the world being caught out and being caught in the trap. Alcohol is embedded in every crevice of our society and for many it's a trusted friend. It has won the confidence of people like you and me who genuinely believe (as I used to) that it adds value to their lives, and that life without it would be deficient. Alcohol is also the cause of inordinate suffering and misery for millions of people who find they can't live with it and can't live without it.

Alcohol is the con trick that is fooling the world. Intelligent, successful, strong-minded people are amongst the most common group to fall for the con and give their trust to alcohol. It's only when you try to get out that the rope tightens, and you realise that you're trapped. With minds yo-yoing between wanting a drink, and trying to stop having one, or just having less, most drinkers mistakenly blame themselves for being weak, and unable to control alcohol. People don't realise that they are victims of a con.

Unless you've read a library of books on addiction, drugs and alcohol lately, then there's a ton of stuff about alcohol that you are completely unaware of, just like I was. And you're a bright person. You're smart. I am too. I've got degrees, I've written books, run businesses and I've raised kids, but I was drawn in by the alcohol con, just like the millions of smart, intelligent, successful people who are still in the trap.

When people try to get out, the con trick keeps them trapped by adding layer upon layer of false confidences and beliefs.

People think they can't live without alcohol, and life would be dull. A few years ago, the very idea of going to a party and not being able to drink would make me feel deprived, even before I got there.

Recently a friend came to stay, and twice before she arrived, I went to my local shops to get some last-minute supplies. Both times I had 'buy wine' on my mental list, because my friend is a drinker. Both times I completely forgot the wine. I ended up texting my partner to ask him to pick up some on the way home from work. A few years ago, I would have gone to the shop to pick up some milk and would have come through the door with two bottles of wine, and completely forgotten the milk. I'm now free, and it feels great.

People talk about 'giving up' alcohol as though there's something to lose, and I appreciate that right now that's what you believe. It's the reason that people are so fearful of facing the problems that alcohol is causing. It's like the abusive partner who beats someone up only to hug them better. We all know that person is manipulative and can't be trusted. The alcohol con is cleverer though, because whereas an abusive lover may shower someone with tangible gifts and benefits, there are literally no benefits to taking alcohol, and you'll get smart to that later in the book.

I use the word 'take' in relation to alcohol interchangeably with the word 'drink', because drinkers *drink* to *take* the drug which is alcohol. Heroin is mostly injected, or smoked, and nicotine is smoked, or vaped. I know that you won't like to think of it that way: *taking* alcohol, but that is what it is. If it makes you recoil, or feel aggrieved, that's okay. You'll find out later that's just your subconscious mind, and it's your subconscious mind that is the real victim of the confidence trick.

Alcohol, and everything that it embodies, is the con artist who has lied and continues to lie to you. Alcohol is the Pied Piper of Hamlyn who plays happy music full of promises of joy. And just like the piper it lures the followers, reeling them in, slowly, subtly, until the point when it's got them, and it's too late. It's not too late for you though, and if you are prepared to get smart with alcohol then you'll be in full control very soon.

Alcohol traps educated, capable, strong-minded people. The only abuser in the alcohol equation is the alcohol itself. It is not us who abuse alcohol, it is alcohol that abuses us.

Alcohol is the loan shark who lends you $20, then demands $30 in repayment, who lends you the $30 to then demand a repayment of $40. It is the loan shark who gives with one hand and takes with both, taking you ever further in debt while you try to get back to being where you were before you started.

It's time to delve into the confidence and trust that we have put in alcohol and to unravel the greatest confidence trick of our time.

Part 1
Smart People Conned

Confidence Trick

"An act of cheating or tricking someone by gaining their trust and persuading them to believe something that is not true"

The Long Boozy Con

EVERY CONFIDENCE TRICK works because it uses psychology as the basis for manipulating belief. When it comes to a con trick, no one is immune, and indeed everybody I know has fallen for the alcohol con trick. Some have fallen further than others, and some have outsmarted it, and got out of the trap that it put us all in.

Alcohol and the industry behind it is the ultimate hustler, and this is how it works.

The confidence trick starts with basic human psychology, and a con trick requires two things to make it work:

- A Con Artist: Alcohol

- A Mark: The Victim, also known as The Drinker

Before you can outsmart a con artist, you need to know how they operate and what's happening.

The Con Artist: Alcohol

THE CON ARTIST IN THIS story is alcohol, or to use its chemical name, ethanol. With no disguise to hide it, our con artist is pure poison, and half a pint of neat alcohol is enough to kill an average sized human.

Alcohol is a very powerful, dangerous and highly addictive drug. Those facts alone are shocking. You would have seen the characterless health pamphlets with data about recommended weekly units of alcohol. They are not written or designed to have any impact, and nowhere do they make it clear that alcohol is:

- A drug

- Powerful

- Dangerous

- Highly addictive

Alcohol is known to damage every single organ in the human body. Why on earth would we want it in our bodies?

At this point we can't talk about the alcohol con artist as purely the ethanol that we drink. It's how the ethanol is used, made into what you drink, branded, advertised, and marketed that massively supports the con. It isn't possible to think of the alcohol con artist and avoid bringing in the advertising industry. I have no intention of starting a war with advertising giants, and they are only doing their job. It is the job of marketing, advertising and sales to persuade customers of the benefits of buying products in any way that is legal. Much of marketing and advertising is about human psychology, playing to people's vulnerabilities and desires.

The infrastructure of the messages communicated by the drinks industry is inextricably woven into the alcohol con. Without any of it, and with clear information and bold health warnings, alcohol would have the same representation as cigarettes do today: no advertising, horrific health warnings, and it would be socially unacceptable.

Let's look at this for a moment. In the 1940s and '50s it is estimated that 80% of men in the UK smoked, and at that time, if you didn't smoke you would have found yourself regularly having to explain why not. Smoking was advertised by brands even using health professionals to promote cigarettes, with the strapline, 'More doctors smoke Camel than any other cigarette'. It was portrayed as being something that sophisticated, interesting and fun-loving people did. Today, with less than 16% of adults smoking, these statistics and marketing messages are unbelievable, but during that time people believed every word of it. Now we know that none of the advertised benefits of smoking were true. Now it's alcohol's turn in the limelight, and the con artist is about to play its mark.

The Mark: The Victim – Us, the Drinkers

THE MARK IS THE TARGET of the confidence trick, and in the case of the alcohol con, the mark is everyone.

It's the con artist's job to understand who the mark is, what they want, and what drives them. The con artist then works out how to play on those desires to achieve what it wants. When that's figured out it's just a case of giving the victim what they want, and the con is set.

The alcohol hustler is so manipulative and persuasive that anybody is a good mark, or victim, for it to gain its confidence. The victim is me. The victim is you. The victim is everybody who drinks.

Let's look at what drinkers want, so we can explore why we all fall for the trick. To understand it we need to start with young drinkers. Because, like me, you were probably in your teens when you were first introduced to alcohol and started drinking.

The Play

AS YOUNG DRINKERS WE all wanted to be part of the good things we saw in society, and to join in with everything everybody else was doing that looked worth doing.

It's only natural that a young person wants to conform to social norms, and in a society where drinking is the norm, this, of course, means drinking. A young drinker wants to fulfil the expectations of their role models, and to experience all the things associated with the positives of becoming an adult and living the good side of life that adults live.

A young person is at a stage of life where they are highly vulnerable to suggestion, let alone when those suggestions come from everywhere, and everyone that they trust. A young person is vulnerable to their desires to fit in, and to prove themselves in the adult world, and so they are vulnerable to their desires for pleasure.

Before you became consciously aware of alcohol, the hustle and the long con had already begun. You would have seen your parents, their friends, and all members of society regularly consuming alcohol in groups, in public places, and at home. In your subconscious mind, you, as a young person, began to associate alcohol as an integrated part of adult life. When we were young, we wanted to fit in with our peers and with the adults we admired, and it's only natural that we wanted the pleasure that we began to perceive them having when they consumed alcohol.

If we'd asked an adult for a drink of alcohol, and were told no, we would have wanted to try it even more. There is nothing like being denied something to make you want it more! That's why willpower is ineffective in outsmarting alcohol, but more on that later.

On a psychological level, young people are hooked by curiosity, and a desire for pleasure and acceptance. These are strong pulls that make it virtually impossible for anyone to resist. At this point young people are bait; alcohol has already won their confidence and the alcohol con is on.

The Rope

"What we take to be true is what we believe ... What we believe determines what we take to be true."

David Bohm, Physicist

THE HUSTLER HAS NOW identified its victim and what they want. It's now time to make the move. The desire has been established out of curiosity and wanting to join in the fun promised by the grown-up world. The young drinker's hopes and fears are clear; alcohol is waiting in the wings to offer the promised land, and to jump in to satisfy the needs and wants that it has placed in the young drinker's path.

The young drinker takes their first sip, and all the hedonistic pleasures that they believed in and wanted are delivered ... or are they?

Take yourself back in time to when you had your first drink 10, 20, or 30 years ago. The first alcoholic drink isn't what it's expected to be, and yours probably wasn't either. The first alcoholic drink experience is disgusting, and a non-drinker finds the smell revolting. You often see them recoil, with a mature drinker at their side laughing at them, with body language that says 'You don't know how good it is,' or 'Oh look at her, isn't she sweet turning up her nose. She just hasn't learned to like it yet.'

This is less true for young drinkers today because the alcohol industry has worked hard to avoid losing any early-stage drinkers who may be put off by the foul taste. Alcoholic drinks are now made sweeter to cater for new drinkers and to make it less difficult for them to navigate those hard days and months of acquiring a taste for what we now know is poison.

So, the first drink tasted horrible and had none of the promised benefits, yet we persevered. Why is this?

From a very young age drinkers are conditioned to believe that there is something very beneficial, grown up and pleasurable about consuming alcohol. As we said, these beliefs come from observing parents and friends, as well as the huge influence of the alcohol advertising industry. There is often little pleasure in these earliest days with alcohol. But the young drinker is so convinced of the benefits of alcohol, and their faith in it is so strong, that a young drinker will work to overcome the initial displeasure. And if they can't do it the first or second time, they'll try even harder.

The initial drink may have left them feeling sick or queasy, dizzy or disorientated, and out of control in a way that felt unpleasant. But the young drinker is still vulnerable, and the benefits that we saw adults and our peers enjoying drew us and other young drinkers further in, and the rope tightened.

Social proof is known to add to the persuasiveness of marketing campaigns. It's a term that covers everything from advertising, reviews, mentions on social media, posters, conversations in the hairdresser, and in the board room, celebrities we see in films, what we see at home, and in our towns and cities. Wherever you look there is social proof that alcohol is amazing, and is the choice for cool, carefree and sophisticated people. It was reported that Heineken paid $45million to have their beer featured in the James Bond film *Skyfall*, and more than 80% of movies have depictions of alcohol use.

When we see those same celebrities making headlines in the rehab centre, we tut, and think, 'What an idiot!'

Just like the alcoholic on a park bench, we close our minds to anything that contradicts what we are determined to believe, and we WANT to believe the alcohol con artist, we really do.

The young drinker has overcome the initial distaste of alcohol that left them dizzy, and disorientated. They have proved themselves to be a fledgling grown-up drinker and are now on their way to becoming a proper drinker and an unwitting alcohol addict.

When I started drinking, and even right up to when I stopped drinking, I didn't understand what alcohol really was, how it worked, or why I kept drinking it even though it was starting to make me miserable.

I didn't know that alcohol was an addictive drug; it wasn't something that I had ever stopped to consider, and I certainly didn't associate reaching into the fridge for a cold glass of Chardonnay at the end of the day as in any way related to addiction. Even the medical profession separates alcohol from other drugs in its service title: *Drug and Alcohol Abuse*. Every part of that title is misleading. We now know that alcohol isn't separate from other drugs, and it abuses the people who are conned into taking it. Alcohol is the abuser.

Let's look at that another way. If you were unfortunate enough to be in a relationship with an abusive partner, would anybody say that you were abusing the relationship, and therefore abusing your partner? Of course not. It would be clear that you would be the victim, and that the abuser is the person dishing out the abuse. It's the same with alcohol. To say that you are abusing alcohol is to present the logic completely back to front. Alcohol is abusing you, and as you'll learn, most of the con relies on back to front logic.

Drugs abuse the victim, pure and simple. Given what we know about the con so far, it should be becoming clear that drinkers don't make a conscious or informed choice to take alcohol. The con is too sophisticated, established and clever. They are lured into a trap.

There is another very clever part of the addiction con. Even if someone knows that a substance is addictive, in the early days of taking the drug they will always think that they are unaffected by it and won't become addicted. Every drug addict on the planet went through a stage when they thought that it didn't apply to them. This is partly because when they first tried the drug, they didn't like it.

No one ever sipped their first drink wanting to be addicted to a chemical that caused them to wake up in the early hours of the morning full of remorse and nausea. No one smoked their first cigarette wanting to be a chain smoker, and no one experimented with heroin wanting to be a heroin addict that their family had given up on.

When people first start drinking alcohol, they take their second, third, and fiftieth drink completely convinced that they won't become addicted. And they conclude this without having any idea of how addiction works. Even when they are addicted, they don't know it, because they are too happy in the middle of the cocoon of the con. They feel safe, they have all the other drinkers with them, and they feel confidence growing in the very substance that is causing them harm.

There are two reasons why people don't know that they have slowly and unwittingly become addicted. Firstly, addiction sits in the subconscious mind, which means that your conscious mind doesn't know anything about it. Secondly, the effects of withdrawal from the first consumption of alcohol are imperceptible. The conclusion: *It can't affect me. I'll never get addicted!*

The minute we had the first drink of alcohol, it began to withdraw from our system. The feelings were barely perceptible, but they were there.

As the alcohol leaves our bodies, it leaves a void. We'll delve a little further into the science behind this later. Essentially, the void was never there before we took the first drink. The void feels like a nagging little itch, or a general feeling of agitation, but it's a tiny feeling and we are largely unaware of it. In fact, it's another part of the confidence trick that this feeling grows very slowly over time, so that we don't notice it developing.

If a non-drinker was to suddenly find themselves with the withdrawal feelings that a regular drinker feels every day, they would feel very snappy, jittery, and on edge. It's not a nice feeling.

The drinking pattern becomes established. We have experienced the initial burst of euphoria from alcohol, and the belief that drinking is beneficial has been reinforced. The next time we have a drink the alcohol gives us a very short burst of euphoria, but it now does more than that.

The drink partially fills the void that was left by the previous drink and therefore we feel a sense of relief which we interpret as pleasure. This pleasure is no more a pleasure than removing a tight article of clothing. It's as pleasurable as getting out of a stiflingly hot car after being stuck in a traffic jam. Filling a void is not pleasurable: the word is 'relief'. Removing a tight item of clothing gives the wearer relief, just the same as getting out of a stiflingly hot car also provides relief. You wouldn't say that ending these things is pleasurable, you're just glad that they've gone away, and you certainly wouldn't go looking to get those feelings back again. But this is what we do when we drink. And we do it again, and again, and again. It's what alcohol does when it fills the void caused by the last drink: it makes the niggling, slightly hungry and unsettling feeling go away. The subconscious mind interprets this relief as being a good thing, and therefore it makes the connection that alcohol is doing us good because it gets rid of a feeling that we don't like.

It's clever. It's devious, and people have no idea it's happening. Understanding the void is fundamental to understanding alcohol addiction and outsmarting alcohol.

A drinker will now seek pleasure and support in the very thing that causes the need for it in the first place. Not satisfied, the con artist ups its game, and the stakes are raised in the form of 'tolerance'. Over time the body becomes tolerant to certain aspects of the poison and the feeling of exhilaration diminishes to virtually nothing. This means that we will drink more as time progresses, chasing the high, and all the while trying to top up the widening void.

The Convincer

FROM THOSE EARLY DRINKS of disgusting displeasure, the alcohol hustle works on the belief system of its mark; the tale that it tells and persuasion that it delivers is second to none. The lure and appeal grow ever greater, while the defences and resistance grow ever smaller. We have turned a corner oblivious of the trap we have fallen into.

We all want to enjoy life safely and fully, and it is human nature, even instinct, to protect ourselves from the bad things in life. But at this point in the con, alcohol has now become a learned response and a trusted vehicle to give ourselves the good things in life that are promised by alcohol.

We begin experiencing alcohol as it was promised, and believe that the relief is genuine pleasure. The fraudster is now our trusted friend and has our complete confidence if not our complete attention yet. But like many abusers the friendship is false, and we now know that the confidence is a lie.

There is still an initial high that we feel somewhere after the first drink or two, or three, depending on tolerance levels that have been built up, but this is followed swiftly by the depressant nature of alcohol as our body starts struggling with the effects of the drug slowing us down, and the stress hormones adrenaline and cortisol are released into our blood stream in an attempt to compensate. This is what causes the horrible 4am anxiety that wakes us up with a pounding heart.

The con artist is now about to prove beyond all reasonable doubt that continuing down this path is guaranteed to work to the victim's benefit. This may take months, years or even decades to fully embed in our mind. Some drinkers may stay at this point all their lives, and they may be the lucky ones that escape without any repercussions or illness. Everybody knows an Aunty Mabel who drank like a fish and smoked like a chimney, and lived until she was 99. Data from a report in the UK, NHS Digital in 2017/8 tells us that about 1 in 4 of us will become dependent on alcohol in our lives. The statistics for the Baby Boomer and Generation X group is of particular concern. People born between 1944 and 1979 are presenting as the highest group with health problems. For people aged between 40-75, 70% of alcohol-related hospital admissions in the UK in 2017 fall within this age group, representing 7.2% of all admissions to hospital in the UK.

As the confidence trick rolls on, after months or years we have become hooked, and the rope has tightened. Alcohol has begun to do so much for us, and we believe it's beneficial in so many ways we never stop to wonder if it really is too good to be true. Drinkers get so far into the con without stopping to question the complete versatility of alcohol and how one substance can do so many different things.

No one questions it. A friend of mine commented once how weird it was that she had a drink when she celebrated something great, and had a drink when she commiserated something bad, 'In fact, I have a drink for pretty much all feelings!' she said.

I never stopped to question how alcohol could relieve boredom one day, relax me the next, remove anxiety at social occasions, make life fun, make me the life and soul of the party, and make me as strong as a lion.

But nor did I associate alcohol with the darker side of the relationship that manifested later in the evening when I talked too much, said too much, thought I was really funny, or was super-sexy and cool. By then drinkers are too drunk to really remember when they're neurotic, or jealous, or angry, or hyper-sensitive to criticism. And they are not likely to remember hurling insults, or falling over, or crying hysterically for hours. Drinkers rarely associate themselves directly with the negative sides of their drinking behaviour because they are never truly there to experience it.

We are drunk, incapable and weakened by the time the alcohol makes us neurotic, jealous, disappointed or angry. When alcohol starts to leave our system at 3 o'clock the following morning, adrenaline starts pumping and our heart rate starts rising as the hangover descends.

These things are dimmed in the background as the void comes back with a new day, and we still believe in the trusted con artist. It might be the next day, or three days, or two weeks later that we reach for another drink: but reach we will.

At this point we are completely convinced by the confidence trick. We've invested our time, beliefs and emotions in alcohol, and the thought of living life without this unquestionable support fills all drinkers with fear and dread.

People are trusting by nature: we've had to be to work with others, to evolve and survive. Therefore, to trust, and be a victim of a confidence trick is to be human, and to be human is to be fallible.

All con tricks have a destructive force at their root, and alcohol is no exception. A confidence trick is designed to manipulate our beliefs. The long alcohol con manipulates our most basic beliefs by feeding on our desire for an existence that is more extraordinary and more meaningful. It is this desire that allows the con to thrive.

In every con trick, there are conflicting mentalities of 'It's too good to be true' and 'I deserve the perceived benefits'. We know that if something's too good to be true, then it probably is, but we're blind to that when it comes to alcohol. Fundamentally, we want it to be true, so we just ignore the fact that it might not be. On the other hand, we're very good at rewarding ourselves with a million different reasons behind 'I deserve alcohol.' And so, we become blind to the obvious conflict between 'too good to be true,' and, 'I deserve a drink,' when it comes to our actions.

We may have even seen others fall into the trap, but we think we're invulnerable.

Drinking alcohol falls clearly into these two mentalities. If you really stop to think about all the things alcohol is supposed to do for you, can it ever make sense? When you eat a banana, you don't do it for fun, or because you're tired, bored, or stressed. We know that bananas are a natural source of flavour and goodness, but even if you love bananas, I doubt you'd be thinking, 'Ooh, I really need to relax. I know, I'll just go get a nice relaxing banana.' If you're feeling hyped about something you wouldn't reach for a banana to regulate your mood.

What about those days when you promise yourself you won't drink, but a voice pipes up, 'I've had a long/hard/boring/stressful/difficult* (delete as appropriate) day, I deserve a drink.'

Despite our deep certainty in our own immunity, or even because of it, we all fall for the psychological manipulation of a confidence trick. And alcohol is a very brilliant confidence trick.

In fact, many confidence tricks are never known to the people who are tricked by them. One of the marvellous ways they work is that when the con falls apart, the person being tricked, the victim, believes that they've been unlucky, and that they have had misfortune when things don't work out as promised. They may believe that the situation they find themselves in is their own fault, or that they're weak, when they are unable to turn the situation to their advantage.

Isn't this so true of alcohol? The whole of society is programmed to see a 'problem drinker' as weak, and as someone who can't control alcohol. One minute a celebrity is a fun, good time drinker, and the next they're being publicly reviled as weak and pathetic.

It's only when a con is revealed that the psychological manipulation is evident. The alcohol con is the same. Drinkers are not weak; in fact, you will see that they are often the most determined and strong-willed of people.

When we invest in something, we calculate the odds that things will turn out as expected. This builds an expectation of an outcome, in psychological terms this is known as 'expectancy'. As any new evidence is received, the initial expectation will affect how we interpret the evidence. This means that despite the 'morning after', the hangovers, the guilt and the shame, we still hold on firmly to our initial expectations of the benefits of alcohol long after they have ceased to exist. Essentially, we are biased to pay attention to information that confirms our initial expectations. Psychologists Neil Rose and Jeffrey Sherman wrote 'Once useful expectancies have developed, our cognitive system is conservative about altering or replacing them. We don't altogether ignore new inputs, that would be maladaptive and stupid, but we err on the side of what we've already decided was true, after all we did a lot of work to get to that point and what we decided was true already can colour how we view the new event. Our prior expectations give us a kind of cognitive road map for how we should look at what's going on.'

Psychologists term this 'tendency' or 'confirmation bias', a predisposition to take in and sift through evidence selectively so we can confirm what we were already expecting to be the case. Society continues to bombard us with confirmation of our beliefs in the benefits of alcohol, even when we have begun to experience strong negatives in our lives.

This psychology is as true of every confidence trick as it is for the con of alcohol. Changing your perception or your memory is easier than changing your behaviour. It's easier to change what we believe about the way we're drinking than to actually quit, particularly when we are looking for evidence to keep our beliefs true. Even if conflicting evidence is received, expectancies tend to be rigid, especially when they've been confirmed in the past. We need to understand more about alcohol and how the con actually works, so that we may see past our bias to confirm what we want to be true. In psychological terms, we need to overcome our confirmation bias.

Our desire to avoid the internal argument of whether to have a drink or not means that we put forward the best possible argument to make sure we get a drink. It's a sort of unconscious equivalent to what a lawyer does when they present evidence in a way that sheds the best possible light on your side of their case.

The Breakdown

THINGS DON'T COMPLETELY fall apart yet, even though the cracks may be beginning to show. At this point in the con, we start want to prove to ourselves that we're in control of our drinking. Drinkers do this in different ways. I used to stop drinking for a few weeks as part of *Dry January* to prove to myself and the world that I didn't have a drink problem. Halfway through the month-long challenge, people would start congratulating me on my resolve, my commitment, and my super-hero strength.

'Yes,' I would nod proudly, 'I'm doing Dry January.'

Then there would be two different kinds of response.

Type one:

'Me too. I had a bit too much vino over Christmas.' Little laugh. 'How's it going?'

'Yeah, fine. You?'

'Yeah, it's okay. Keep up with the distractions, you know anything to stop thinking about a cold glass of wine ...?'

'Yeah, me too.' Smiles. 'Can't wait for February though. The wine's waiting in the fridge!'

Relaxes, 'I can't wait either. My gin's in the cupboard.' Laughs.

'See you then! Keep up the good work!'

Type Two:

'Yes,' I would nod proudly, 'I'm doing Dry January.'

'Oh, you're not! Why? Are you mad! I could never do that. I like my wine too much!' Nudges, winks, laughs very loudly.

I scuttle off feeling stupid.

Just think about it for a second, what would you think if there was a *Banana-free January*, and hordes of people were signing up to it. You'd probably wonder if there was a banana shortage. If they carried a health warning, you'd never eat a banana again, and you would certainly wonder why bananas were the focus of such attention.

Now imagine those same two conversations being about bananas. This is what you would hear:

'I'm doing Banana-free January.'

'I had a few too many bananas over Christmas.'

'Are you mad! I could never do that. I like my bananas too much!'

The chances are that if you need to stop drinking for a month to prove that you don't have a problem, then you probably do. Would you need to give up bananas for a month, or peas, or carrots? Of course not, because they're good for you, and I doubt that you consume them to excess. You're also not addicted to bananas, because they're not addictive, and if they were toxic and poisonous you would never have one again.

You may also have tried to control your drinking in other ways. I know that I did all of the following things at different times: only allow yourself a certain number of drinks at a time, or only drink on certain days of the week, or call a halt to drinking at a certain time. No doubt you managed it for a while, as I did, again feeling noble and proud as you declined a round of drinks, or smilingly placed your hand over your half empty glass that you're nursing.

Then something would have happened. And it could have been anything. It could be an event where you felt that you needed to drink, or one of those particularly hard days when you thought you deserved a drink, or any number of other reasons why the little voice in your head piped up and shouted, 'I deserve it ... I need it.'

When we try to stop drinking or cut down, we may tell ourselves that it's okay to drink at the weekend, or it's okay not to drink wine but to drink gin, or it's okay to drink every other day, or it's okay to drink every day but just a small amount. Whatever we decide, what we are doing is trying to make ourselves feel better by changing the rules of the game. Ultimately, these methods of trying to control consumption won't work. The natural progression of addiction is that over time we will always drink more, and not less.

And we're back where we were. If we're lucky we are drinking the same amount as before, but often we'll find that we are drinking a little more.

Something else that we might try is to behave differently when we've been drinking. Maybe our drinking behaviour has caused problems with work colleagues, or a loved one. Maybe we've got ourselves into dangerous or illegal situations. We'll tell ourselves that we will be more controlled, and that it will all be okay because this time it will be different. You'll know that you are a capable person, and that when you decide to do something, you'll do it. You may tell yourself that, 'This time I won't be overly critical of ...', or 'This time I'll not flirt with ...', or 'This time I'll not get into a fight', or 'This time I won't get angry.' This is probably the saddest and most soul destroying of all things to try to do.

Alcohol is a depressant, and this doesn't mean that it makes you miserable, although it often does that the day after. Alcohol depresses the central nervous system so much that it results in impairments such as slurred speech, unsteady movement, disturbed perceptions, and an inability to react quickly. Mentally, alcohol reduces our ability to think rationally, lessens inhibitions, and distorts judgement. Given this information, it makes it extremely difficult to change drunken behaviour; because we are not thinking rationally, our inhibitions are non-existent, and our emotions are going haywire.

The only way to behave differently is not to get drunk, and the only way to guarantee that is not to drink. But that is easier said than done. I spent over ten years trying to adapt my behaviour when I was drunk. It was like rolling a dice. Sometimes I'd win and sometimes I'd lose, but on balance it just didn't work.

By trying to cut down or stop drinking altogether, drinkers are like a fish on a hook and the more we struggle, the more the line tightens, and the deeper the hook embeds.

Drinking alcohol then becomes a personal problem that we begin to realise can't solve. When we realise that we have little control over alcohol, our stress levels rise, and we become concerned, and anxious about the hold that drinking alcohol has on us. That's when, paradoxically, we're more likely to turn to alcohol for the perceived support that it gives us. Because what happens when we feel stressed? We have a drink. At this point we are pulled even further into the con, and we become more reliant on alcohol.

The good news is that you have everything that you need to break free from the con artist, and layer by layer, like unpeeling an onion, you are already on that journey. You have ventured into the unknown many times before in your life. You have done things for the first time not knowing whether you could, and not knowing what the outcome would be. This is just another of those things.

The con is exposed, and once you have seen it for what it is, you can never un-see it. The mask is off.

It is a hard truth that none of the regular people like you and me, who drink alcohol, know anything about how drugs work, why they keep us coming back for more, and how the process of addiction works.

Your eyes have now begun to open.

I didn't know much of what I have learned since I stopped drinking in 2016. I had my first alcoholic drink, aged eight, at a family gathering. I remember laughing and crying myself to sleep. If my parents had known that the thimbles-full of wine they let me have was an addictive drug, they most certainly wouldn't have given it to me. I went on to start drinking occasionally, and then socially at around age 16, then I progressed to drinking to keep up with the boys at university, to drinking and partying at weekends with friends when I started working. That went on to drinking after work with my husband, to drinking alone as a single mother. As my friend said, 'I drink when something goes well, and I drink when something goes badly. In fact, I drink when anything happens!' Like many others, I was lulled into a false sense of security, because most of the people I knew admitted to drinking for those reasons too.

And the bitter truth is that we are all drinkers who are addicted to the addictive drug that is alcohol.

Try telling a room full of people who have just arrived at a party that there is no alcohol, but plenty of soft drinks, and watch the reaction. It's a little different to being told there are no sausage rolls but there's plenty of food, isn't it?

One of the things that I find completely baffling is that there is so much money spent on alcohol awareness resources, how many units you should have in a week etc, but I don't remember seeing anywhere a clearly spelt out message that alcohol is a drug and if you take it you'll likely get addicted. One of the major problems is that even the support organisations and general practitioners don't really understand the deceit and ingenious trappings of the alcohol confidence trick, and they don't communicate with people anywhere near as powerfully as the advertising giants who are selling alcohol.

This book is about being enlightened and empowered to finally make the choice that you never had before, and it's about having the tools and understanding to be as smart with alcohol as you are with other parts of your life.

Crisis or Opportunity

IT TOOK A PERSONAL crisis for me to decide to stop drinking alcohol. My partner told me I had to, or he would leave. It was as simple as that. The problem was that I didn't know how to stop because I had tried to several times before.

I always managed it for a while but then I would either forget how bad things had been, or I would tell myself that a drink or two wouldn't do any harm, or I would find a glass in my hand without even making a conscious decision to start drinking again. I never actually decided on any of those occasions that I needed to, or wanted to, stop drinking permanently. If I had, the thought of it would have been so unacceptable that it would have barely registered in my consciousness.

After the ultimatum, I took a long walk and came to the conclusion that I needed to stop drinking, and that I probably needed to stop drinking permanently. It may have been an obvious conclusion to an outsider, but the subconscious mind is incredibly powerful, and mine didn't want to admit that it had been so wrong. I couldn't see any alternative, and I now realise that there was no alternative. There was one big problem though. I didn't know how I was going to do it.

What should have been easy, to just stop doing something, began to look like it was completely impossible. I was and still am a high achiever. I started my first business at the age of 20, just a few years after graduating from a top London University with a biochemical degree. I was completely confident in my abilities to set goals, to achieve them, and to learn anything I didn't know along the way.

But my learning experiences with alcohol had proved different, and all my capabilities, confidence and strong will had failed to get me the outcome I wanted.

I am now on the other side of the alcohol trap, and if I had known then what I know now I would have happily walked away from the con artist never to consider it again. But I am here sharing my knowledge, training and research with you so that you too can outsmart alcohol.

There is so much that I did not know about alcohol. For example, I did not know that the awful feelings that I had the day after drinking were because of alcohol withdrawal. I understood the obvious physical effects because I'd had them many times before. I understood the headache, and on a particularly heavy night the nausea. I understood that if I had drunk a bottle of wine after work that the next day I might feel a little jaded. What I didn't know was that the feelings of guilt and shame and misery, and just feeling fed up were all caused by alcohol as well.

I used to wake up on a Saturday or Sunday morning , and the first thing that would come into my head was the question , 'What did I do or say last night?' and the guilt and awful feelings of anguish would come before I even had the answer. I even managed to convince myself that the nit-picking, niggly criticisms and nasty comments that I hurled around after a bottle or two of wine came from some angry inner child busting to get out. I thought that there was something wrong with me and that drink brought deep-seated issues to the surface.

I have not had any feelings of guilt or shame or misery since I took my last drink. I never wake up in the morning wondering what I did. And I never lay in bed with a headache as fragments of the previous night come back to me. I have not been angry or lost my temper in years. I don't nit-pick and I don't criticise. If I have something to say I'll say it clearly and with confidence because I mean it. That alone has been a wonderful and freeing gain. I have my mornings and I love them. I used to say that I was an evening person and not a morning person , but now I realise it was alcohol that was the evening influence that wrecked the mornings; now that I'm completely free I get to bed at a reasonable time and I get up early to embrace the day feeling great .

I did not know that alcohol is addictive. Seriously! For years, I didn't know that. I didn't think of myself as someone who regularly took a lot of a highly addictive drug. Had I known that, and had my friends known that, then I guarantee we would have had some open discussions about that at some point. But we didn't, and I am talking about university-educated people who sit round a table, sharing food, getting drunk on a Friday night, week after week, people who debate the issues of the day. And yet never was anything ever said about the fact that we were all regularly consuming an addictive drug. And the reason that it was never discussed wasn't because we were avoiding the issue, because every other issue was thrown up and discussed at those dinner parties. But not once ever, in all the conversations we had about when we drink, and why we drink, and how we drink, did anybody mention that we were consuming a highly addictive drug. And the reason for that is because none of us knew.

We are well aware that somebody who uses heroin is a heroin addict, and we understand somebody who smokes cigarettes is addicted to nicotine, but it seems to be only the minority who have made the connection between consuming alcohol and alcohol addiction.

How We Learn

THERE IS A PROCESS that we all go through when we grow from one place of learning to another. It is the process of how we get better at anything in life. And we always need to start the learning and change process before we are completely ready.

This means that the first decision when we want things to be different is the decision to do something. There is no need to know what to do or how to do it. The first decision is to do something, and that something is to learn more. That is probably why you are here reading this book. You have already made the decision to learn how to solve an alcohol problem, so let's take a look at the learning process so that you can navigate the rest of your journey with ease.

The process that we go through to learn something new is as true of learning to cook, drive a car, or manage people as it is of learning to take back control and stop drinking.

Firstly, in all these situations we do not know with absolute certainty that we're going to be able to succeed. How can we when we've not done something before? That is the nature of learning. Where we have seen others before us successful, and we're told that we have the capability, we may be confident that we can learn the new skills.

When it comes to alcohol problems though, we often lack the confidence to try to change because we have witnessed it being impossible or very difficult for others, and we also have experience of failing at controlling drinking in the past.

Let's explore this in more detail. At one point in your life you couldn't walk. At one point you couldn't talk. In your lifetime you may have learned to drive a car. In your lifetime you would have learned and developed in all kinds of ways as a result of information and learning. In all likelihood you will have gone through the four stages of learning to become competent many times before.

The 'four stages of learning' relates to the psychological states involved in the process of progressing from not being able to do something to being competent, and it is relevant to every area of our lives. You can think of it as being unaware, and asleep, and through learning becoming aware and fully awake.

You would have heard of the phrase *you don't know what you don't know*. The problem is that we are often unaware of what we don't know, and we work on intuition, which comes from the subconscious.

We rely on intuition to do what is necessary and this doesn't always serve us well. Unfortunately, when it comes to alcohol, unless we are prepared to look at the situation and start asking questions, we will remain stuck, wrapped in the con for the rest of our lives. Let's look at the four stages of learning.

STAGE 1 UNCONSCIOUS INCOMPETENT: FROZEN

Before we set out to learn or change anything, we are what is called 'unconsciously incompetent'. Basically, this means that we don't know what we don't know. At this point we don't even know that we need to learn anything, and we think everything we know is all there is to know.

We may have been doing something for a long time, and we think that we are pretty good at it. In the alcohol con, we are *Frozen* when we believe that we know everything that we need to know about alcohol, and that our drinking isn't a problem. At this point we are stuck or frozen in our knowledge and our ability to change. And so, nothing changes. It's like being frozen in time, not moving forwards, but just going round in circles, repeating the same behaviour, day after day, month after month, year after year. When it comes to alcohol, it's not just us who is frozen in time, most of our peers, our friends and family are as well.

You are here reading this book because you know that what you have been doing around alcohol until now hasn't worked. Maybe it worked for a while, but it didn't stick, and you found yourself back at square one.

You are ahead of millions of successful, smart people around the world who remain stuck, because you are moving on to Stage 2. The first step to becoming unfrozen is to recognise that there is a blind spot in your knowledge around alcohol and addiction that is affecting your success at getting the changes in your life that you want. We need to recognise that we have a problem, then we can learn how to solve it.

STAGE 2 CONSCIOUS INCOMPETENT: FLOUNDERING

At stage 2 we are now aware that something isn't right with us and alcohol, and now we set about starting to try to solve our growing drink problem.

Take the example of learning something new in a class. Imagine you are in a yoga, badminton, or swimming class. Imagine that you are swimming a length, taking a shot or doing a yoga move. You will do the move to the best of your ability using the knowledge that you have and the skills you have acquired. But it is only when the class teacher comes over and highlights what you are doing wrong, and how to do it differently, that you then move to the state of becoming 'consciously incompetent'. Up until that point, as far as you were aware you were doing everything correctly. Now your bubble has burst, and you realise that you weren't that good after all. You may start to feel determined to get better, or enthusiastic to learn more, but you may also feel a bit deflated, because you thought you were doing okay.

When it comes to alcohol we need to get to this point so that we can be aware that there is a problem to solve, and we can't do that if we don't recognise that we are in fact addicted to alcohol.

When we try to control alcohol ourselves, we often start by inventing all kinds of rules for ourselves. We try dry months, we try not drinking at certain hours of the day, or on certain days of the week. We find that what we do works for a while, and usually fails. We wrongly conclude that it's us who are incapable of controlling ourselves and our problem. We don't consider the fact that maybe we have the wrong information, and we need to learn how to solve our problem properly.

We are well and truly floundering at this stage in the learning process; it's frustrating and soul destroying, and the problem with addiction is that no matter how hard you try you will not be able to succeed if you're using the wrong method.

It's as hopeless a venture as trying to stop the tide coming in on a beach. When I was a child I played on the beach with my brother, and we would try to stop the tide coming in by building a fortress around our sandcastles. Even as a child I knew that failing to stop the tide had no bearing on my capabilities as a person, my strength of will, or my intellect, and it had everything to do with the fact that I was facing a force that was unstoppable – the incoming tide!

When we use the wrong method to stop drinking alcohol, we question our capabilities and strength because we can't understand why we fail. With the right learning and the right method, the force of alcohol addiction is stoppable. And that is great news!

The fact is that stopping drinking is easier than learning to swim well, playing badminton or being a yogi, because there are no specific skills needed to stop or to control drinking, whereas the yoga, swimming and badminton students all require skills to perfect their craft.

With the alcohol con, it is purely a case of knowing how to walk away from the incoming tide, and that requires no skill at all. What it does require is an awareness of the futility of the method being used up until now, and an awareness of what to do instead.

When I realised that I was floundering in my attempts to control my drinking, I knew that what I'd been doing hadn't worked for me, and I knew that I didn't know what to do to make it work. This open mindedness is essential for all learning. Our human minds are amazing, and we have the capacity to learn and evolve throughout an entire lifetime. Neuroplasticity is the term that describes the huge adaptability of our brains.

The next stage in the journey is to acquire the learning needed to make the necessary changes.

STAGE 3 CONSCIOUS COMPETENCE: FIXATED

At stage 3 in every learning path, we may have learned a new skill, but it takes a huge amount of effort to apply our new learning correctly and consistently. We would have changed our behaviour, and we will be doing things differently, but it is a conscious effort.

You remember when you first learned to drive a car? You would have been thinking about every gear change and every minute shift with the steering wheel. You would have been very conscious and mindful every second of what you were doing. If you relaxed and forgot about what you were doing for a second, you may have had a jolt, and worried that you'd made a mistake, or been fearful of slipping up.

When we follow the correct method to learn to take back control of our thinking from alcohol, we transition right through Stage 3 and onto Stage 4 without stopping. It is immediate, and it is absolutely normal to go from Stage 2 and bypass Stage 3 completely.

The problem occurs when we follow the wrong method and stay at Stage 3 forever. If we constantly need to be alert and concentrate on not doing something (in this case not drinking alcohol), and not making a mistake, that is highly stressful, that is not a good way to live.

If we try to control our drinking by abstaining or trying to use willpower, we stay fixated on alcohol. We need to go to endless AA meetings, or set ourselves a constant barrage of rules to live by.

My method is about freedom, having complete control and living a thriving life without alcohol causing an endless cycle of misery.

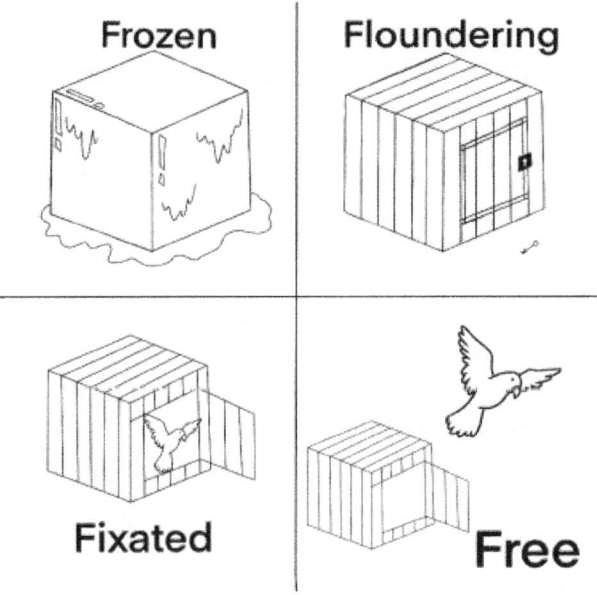

| Frozen | Floundering |
| Fixated | Free |

STAGE 4 UNCONSCIOUS COMPETENCE: FREE!

In Stage 4 the unconscious competent person can practice their new skills and behaviour with ease, and it becomes second nature. Change has been embedded deep within the subconscious: that means for you, as someone who may be struggling with alcohol - freedom!

Freedom means that alcohol has become insignificant in your life and you are back in control without the con artist breathing down your neck and manipulating your thoughts and beliefs. That freedom is an amazing feeling.

These four stages from 'frozen' to 'freedom' are applicable to all people who are caught in the alcohol trap. It is the method that is used between Stages 2 and 3 which makes the difference as to whether a person can become fully relaxed and free in Stage 4, or remains fixated in Stage 3 with the fear of going back to Stage 2 and floundering once again.

The key to making the difference is to fully learn about the alcohol con and how it works, and not to simply change your behaviour through grit and determination, and hope it works.

Part 2
Smart People Learn

Let's Get Smart

IF ALCOHOL AND EVERYTHING it represents is a con, and is the cause of drink problems and addiction, how can we see through the con to get to the other side and solve our problem?

You are going through the process right here, right now. Let me break it down for you.

Recognise that there is a problem and want it solved. You must want to get away from the problem more than you want to stay with it.

Learn...learn...learn about alcohol and how you fell for the con. Understanding is key.

Challenge everything you have ever known about alcohol and approach the coming pages with an open and inquisitive mind.

Remove the fear of both change and success and build your self-efficacy – you can do it!

Challenge and then change the beliefs that the con planted in your subconscious mind.

Never see alcohol in the same way again. Once you have seen through a con trick, you can never unsee it!

I am assuming that you have ticked the box for point 1 above, and that is why you are reading this book. We have already talked about how young drinkers, and indeed all drinkers, fall for the con. Your learning process has begun. Let's continue to expose and unravel the con so that if you choose to, you can walk away to freedom.

It is not surprising that alcohol was rated as the most damaging drug on the planet in a study led by Professor Nutt in the UK. You read earlier that on a scale where 100 is total damage and zero is no harm, alcohol scored 72 out of 100, 17 points more than heroin, which scored 55 out of 100, while cocaine scored 54 out of 100. Alcohol is also the second most addictive drug on the planet after heroin.

If this drug is the most damaging drug and the second most addictive drug on the planet then it is highly likely that someone like me who consumed it regularly for 30 years is going to become addicted and is going to suffer harm as a result.

One of the reasons that alcohol scores so highly for 'harm' is because of the damage that alcohol causes to others close to us: our family, partners and children. If we are wine o'clock or evening drinkers and consume half a bottle or more of wine every night, we never spend a sober evening with our families, and our children never see us sober in an evening. This means we are never seen as we truly are. All our loved ones see is a stressed person coming in through the door diving for a drink, putting everyone and everything second, and thus perpetuating the image of alcohol being necessary as a part of life.

These are some of the effects that alcohol has on us. Alcohol:

- Slows our speech and affects our hearing, so that we can't distinguish sounds or the direction of sounds

- Affects our ability to see clearly, and to taste and smell

- Breaks down our immune system, making us less resistant to diseases, and destroys brain cells

- Weakens our heart and its efficiency at pumping blood throughout our body

- Destroys the lining of our stomach and weakens our muscles

- Causes diabetes, seven different types of cancer, liver and kidney disease

- Weakens bones because alcohol limits the body's ability to absorb calcium

- Causes irritation in our intestines, and leads to nausea, vomiting, and diarrhoea

- Ruins our self-esteem, undermines our confidence, and leads to anxiety and depression.

If you're anything like I was, I could tell you that alcohol is a highly toxic, cancer-causing poison that kills over three million people every year, and it wouldn't make any difference – you'd still pour your next glass.

If I told you that it affects your central nervous system, affecting reason, judgement, eyesight, hearing, and motor function, that probably wouldn't make any difference either.

The truth is that most people who drink alcohol do know that it is harmful, but we also think that this harm is abstract, the damage won't happen to us, and that any risk is worth the huge benefits to be gained. But these benefits are an illusion, and they are the same illusion of all drugs.

We are in a growing pandemic of alcohol addiction, and the people most affected are smart and capable: they are people like me and people like you. As the founder of The Alcohol Coach I hear the real life stories of the people who reach out to me – people whose partners have walked out, people who have lost access to their children, people frightened, and desperate to get on with their lives without being dragged down in a cycle of drinking. I also hear about people who are scared of failing and of what life will be like without alcohol. I hear about people who fear socializing, being accepted, and not being fun anymore.

People used to think that inhaling nicotine was fun too.

When these people learn the truth, they realise that it is the ingenious nature of the alcohol con that is the source of problems, and the way out is to get smart.

Science of Willpower

OUR CONSCIOUS MIND accounts for approximately 5% of the whole mind, with our subconscious mind accounting for a staggering 95%. That makes our subconscious mind a powerhouse, and it is the ruler of everything that we have ever learned and everything that we have learned to believe. All our conditioning and the majority of what we do on a daily basis is driven by our subconscious mind. This includes all the things that we haven't learnt to do well, based on inaccurate assumptions or conclusions.

There are too many things that we do regularly for us to be able to keep everything in our conscious mind. It is just not possible. Our conscious mind is very good at making decisions and deciding strategy, but the rest of our mind is where all the work gets done on a daily basis. The conscious mind is like the board room, and the subconscious mind is the rest of the staff in the organisation beneath. To enable everything to function smoothly once something has been learned (correctly or incorrectly), and usually after much repetition, all activities, beliefs, and capabilities get put into our subconscious.

We just know how to drive a car, ride a bike, and walk once we have learned how to do it, and whether we are good at it or not, we settle into our learned way of doing things unless something wakes us up to a need, and we learn something new. Without feedback our learning essentially becomes frozen in time, and if we have learned things incorrectly, we settle into being an unconscious incompetent. Our subconscious mind contains every thought, every feeling, and every behavioural pattern from our past, and you may find it surprising to learn that every decision we make today is largely based on what we've done, learned or concluded in the past. And that means that our subconscious is making decisions for us.

The purpose of the subconscious mind in this context is to help us by making us happy and protecting us from harm. In this job our subconscious is very efficient. We have evolved to survive, and it is our ability to survive that has bought us to where we are today as a species. But what happens when our subconscious mind is conned?

Our subconscious is not always right. Alcohol hijacks our natural biology by short-circuiting our reward and learning cycles, as we will discover later.

The key point here is that we have learned by clever manipulation to become addicted to alcohol in our subconscious mind, and addiction to alcohol is 90% psychological.

When we wake up in the morning deciding to not drink that day, week, or ever again, we make the decision in our conscious mind, but our subconscious mind is the ruler of addiction. This starts a battle of wills between our small conscious mind, and our powerhouse of a subconscious mind. Our natural biological response will always seek homeostasis, or balance, and this disagreement between a decision not to drink and our subconscious learning which says we should drink, causes something called cognitive dissonance. This is essentially a 'thinking disagreement', which sets things out of balance. It's also stressful in itself, and who wants an argument raging in their head?

Our natural biological reaction is to want balance, and to have warring thoughts of not drinking and wanting to drink is stressful. All of my clients at The Alcohol Coach tell me that at different times they drink to alleviate stress, and to feel relaxed. We are therefore more likely to drink when we're stressed, and so it is easy to understand that our preconditioned learning and beliefs will win, and we'll retract our decision to not drink. We give up, cave in, reach for the bottle, and feel like a failure.

Then when we have the drink, the relief we feel from the withdrawal and the end of dissonance is interpreted by our subconscious as being beneficial, and our belief that alcohol is both necessary and pleasurable is once more reinforced.

The childhood game that my brother and I played by the sea took a lot of willpower too.

As the water advanced with the incoming tide, a slow trickle would begin to break through the walls of our sand castle defences. At first the trickle was so slight that we left it, but then we would notice that the barrier that we had erected was eroding as the water continued to push its way through. We would build up our sand wall again, determined and hopeful that we would keep the water back.

The effort and determination we put into our defences was enormous. And as you know our efforts were in vain. If King Canute couldn't hold back the tide, me and my eight-year-old brother weren't likely to!

As the water advanced, we would get our buckets and be ankle-deep in the water inside our castle walls as we threw bucketful after bucketful of water out, shouting instructions to each other and as we ran faster and faster trying to keep the tide out. We would be bucketing faster and faster and losing ground quicker and quicker. It was hard work!

This is what happens when we try to control alcohol using the wrong method. When we use the wrong method, try as we might, we find ourselves failing, and then we start to tell ourselves that we're not strong willed enough, and that we didn't try hard enough.

Thinking and feeling that way is self-defeating. Playing on those feelings, we will learn later, is one of the masterful plays of the alcohol con artist. But, have no fear, because we are outsmarting it.

Were we, as children, weak because we didn't build our defences better? Did we have a character defect? Or did the tide advance because that's what the tide always does? The only way that we could have beaten the tide was to not be there in the first place.

The problem with alcohol is alcohol. And you and I never stood a chance. The nature of addiction is that we have to consume more of it more often in order to stem the tide, and even then it is only temporary.

Every time alcohol is used to fill the void that the previous alcoholic drink filled, the void becomes slightly bigger and more alcohol is needed to fill it the next time. The results being that the void is never filled, and drinker is never at the same level that they were before they started drinking. Just like our wonderful fortress was never as magnificent as it was before the tide started advancing.

This book is not about being helpless in the face on an incoming tide, or being a victim and powerless to alcohol. It is the opposite, and it is about changing the way you think and feel about alcohol so that you can get your power back and take control.

You have now learned that willpower is not the way to outsmart alcohol. If alcohol is to lose its hold over us, we need to literally change our minds about it. That is what you are learning here. Everything that you are reading is part of the process in changing the way you think and feel about alcohol.

Drinking is Stressful

EVERYBODY HAS CHALLENGING times in their lives and everybody has situations that are stressful. Some people are better able to cope with life's issues than others. However well you cope with life stresses, drinking will only serve to increase your levels of stress.

Consider all the aspects in your life as a circular pie, and the different things that cause you stress are slices of the pie. There will be money issues, health issues, relationship issues – maybe a divorce, or it could be that you're unhappy in your marriage, or that you are alone and wish to find somebody in your life; there may be stresses of children and their health, schooling, or friendships; there may be stresses from a holiday or not having a holiday, the car breaking down, a toothache, or somebody moaning about the dinner you've just cooked.

There will be plenty of things to put in that pie that will be causing you stress. Now add alcohol to the equation. When we first start drinking in the early days, we'll come home from work, and work will be on our minds. We may be a little stressed about it and we walk into our home to find yesterday's washing up, and we may or may not find a spouse and children. We reach for that glass at wine o'clock because we have grown accustomed to believing that this glass of wine is going to help us relax and remove the stress that we're feeling. Fast forward six months, and there's another element of stress in our 'stress pie' and that slice in our pie is called alcohol. Now when we're driving home from work, we'll be thinking about the glass of wine that we're going to have out of the fridge at wine o'clock when we walk through the door. Once that idea is planted in our brain our subconscious will do everything in its power to make sure we get what we want. That is the job of the subconscious mind. The subconscious mind is there to protect us, and it is there to help us get what we think we need.

The subconscious mind, however, is unable to distinguish between what we want and what we really need or should have, and it is flawed. Nevertheless, the subconscious mind will help us to get the alcohol that it believes is beneficial to us.

And you will probably feel a niggling, nagging stress in the pit of your stomach when you begin to think about having a drink. You may be thinking about a drink at lunchtime, but you know that you can't have one because of the confines and restraints of work, so you put the feeling aside. You put the thought aside and you look forward to it for later that evening. When you get in through the door the feeling of the need for alcohol will grow larger until it's the first thing you do when you walk in through the door. The alcohol piece of the stress pie grows bigger.

The timeline is different for different people based on a variety of reasons, but the alcohol slice of your stress pie will inevitably grow, just like the tide will continue to come in and more and more buckets of water are needed just try and keep on top of the problem.

As the addiction takes hold, alcohol becomes one of the main sources of stress in our lives, and the irony is that in order to deal with the stress that alcohol is causing, we drink more, thinking we're alleviating the problem. And all the time we're making the problem worse.

When we realise that alcohol is a problem in our lives and we want to cut down, or stop drinking completely, that starts another cycle of stress, because it's at the moment when we realise we're trapped and try to get away that we realise we can't. Like a fish caught on a line we start to try to wriggle free, and all the time we become more tightly caught.

When I decided that there might be a problem for me with alcohol, I tried to do all kinds of things to manage the problem. I used all the resources that I used in other areas of my life – I used determination, I made plans, I gave myself rules to live by. For example I said that when I went out for a night I'd stop drinking at 10pm, I made the decision to not drink during the week, to never drink before 6pm, to never open the second bottle of wine, to not drink alone, to only buy mini bottles from the shop ...

I made all those decisions over the years, and they all fell by the wayside. They all failed. Nothing I did lasted for long, and I was always back to square one. That's stressful, and the way alcohol made me feel emotionally when I woke up after the parties that I couldn't remember was also stressful.

Imagine a car alarm going off right now outside the window where you are. Imagine it going on and on in the background. Thirty minutes passes and it's still

73

going ... one hour, four hours. You start to get agitated, maybe you go to the window and look out, hoping that just by doing that it would stop. As you get more wound up it's occupying more of your thoughts, and you just can't concentrate on anything else. You find yourself snapping at people, and you're feeling stressed by the car alarm. Finally, the alarm stops. It is silent.

How do you feel? Do you feel happy? Is this having fun? Or do you feel relieved, and sigh with relief that the gnawing annoyance has been silenced?

You feel relieved because the source of your stress is gone.

Now, here's the question:

Would you turn the car alarm back on again just so that you can have the relief of turning it off again?

Alcohol causes the release of stress and anxiety hormones adrenaline and cortisol, which remain in our system at a raised level after we have been drinking. When we take the next drink we numb that feeling, fooling the brain into thinking that alcohol relaxes us, when in fact we are turning off the car alarm just to turn it back on again.

The Science of Cravings

ALCOHOL HIJACKS OUR natural biology and it hijacks and cons our natural motivation, reward and learning process. For millions of years humans have evolved, survived and prospered based on an effective system of motivation, reward and learning.

If this system had not been in place the human race would no longer be here. So, what has this got to do with alcohol addiction? It has everything to do with it.

Humans are lazy. Every species will do the minimum that is required to survive. To ensure our survival, humans are equipped with dopamine. Dopamine is a neurotransmitter that is released by the brain to motivate us to get what we think we need to survive.

When a Stone Age person had a coconut, bashed it with a stone and released the milk, she had a surge of good feeling. The next time she wanted milk she would climb a tree to get the coconut knowing that when she grasped it she would get a surge of good feeling. If she carried on doing the same thing day after day that feeling would get less and less each time, and yet she still wants that surge of good feeling. So, she is motivated to do more. Possibly she will go in search of different food further afield, or rather than bashing the coconut with a stone she would build an axe, which is more effective, and once more she would get that surge of good feeling. She would then associate that surge of good feeling with getting something of value that she needs, and she would move on pushing herself further and further each time. This process underpins our evolution and achievements as a species, and it works very well.

The problem is when alcohol hijacks this natural process. The surge of good feeling that the Stone Age woman gets is from dopamine, and when we consume alcohol, which is a drug, it also has the effect on our brains of releasing the neurotransmitter dopamine. Our natural biology then associates consuming alcohol with getting something that we think we need to survive, and from that moment, we're hooked into the con. If this weren't bad enough, the law of diminishing returns is also in operation here. Our natural biology is not satisfied with us consuming the same amount of alcohol, because in order to motivate us to do more, the initial level of dopamine high reduces, and so we need to drink more and more, always getting less and less of an effect.

Unlike the Stone Age woman with a coconut, we don't go further afield looking for something different, or developing new tools. We go to the fridge and open the second bottle of wine looking for that surge of feeling from alcohol. But the void is still growing, and as we chase the elusive high trying to feel normal, we are getting further and further away from normal. As time passes, alcohol drags us lower and lower, so we never even get close to how we felt before we ever started drinking it.

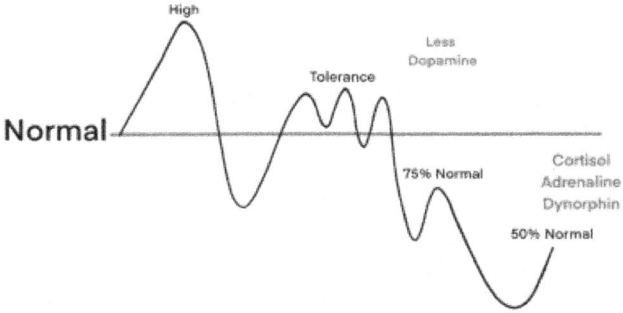

Drinking to Feel Normal

Every drinker consumes alcohol to feel the way they did before they ever had a drink. Every drinker plays with the con artist hoping to feel the peace of mind they felt before they had ever met. You now know different, and to gain peace of mind you need to cut of the supply.

The great news is that within 7 to 12 days of ending the relationship with the con artist your stress levels will have dropped significantly, your body will be calmer and less agitated, and you will be bouncing back to your 'real' normal.

We now understand what motivates us to drink alcohol, but how does a craving manifest and what can we do about it?

The answer lies in the different areas of our brain.

When we decide not to drink and to cut off the alcohol supply, different parts of our brain begin to react. When we understand this, we can learn how to respond.

To explain what happens we will use an analogy, and you can refer to the diagram to help.

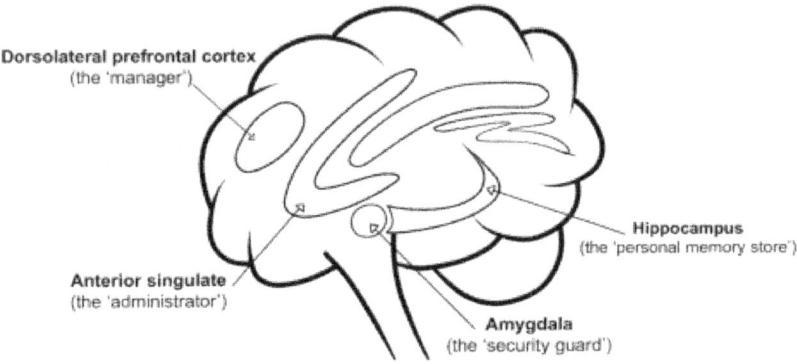

Consider your brain as a small business. This is a brain role play, so let's assign some roles. We have: the manager (that's you – your conscious, decision-making mind), the administrator, who manages the records (the part of your subconscious that organises all your memories and beliefs), and the security guard, whose job it is to keep everybody safe and happy.

As the manager you decide that there is to be no alcohol allowed on the premises. You are completely determined about this. It's just historical that alcohol had always been allowed before. No one had ever questioned it, and alcohol had always been in ready supply.

As the alcohol stores level drops, the security guard notices the computer console in the office as it starts to flash red. This isn't normal, and the guard thinks that there must be something wrong. He sends an alert through to the administrator, to say get more alcohol, there's been a breach.

The administrator fires off a text to the manager (that's you), and says, 'We've got a problem. The alcohol levels have gone down, there has been a breach and the security guard says we need to top them up otherwise there's going to be a problem.'

You politely reply saying that there is a change in policy and that's not going to happen – from now on the business is an alcohol-free zone.

Meanwhile the security guard notices that stocks are sinking lower and lower, and there are early signs of unrest. He puts an urgent call in to the administrator saying, 'Get more alcohol!'

The administrator is slightly baffled, so goes to access the records and files. What happened last time there was a problem? The records show that the manager's request to stop all alcohol purchases is unprecedented. This hasn't happened before, or if it did it was a disaster. So, the administrator sends another message up to you, this one more persuasive, and just for extra measure the files/memories are sprinkled with dopamine to give the message extra motivation for action.

Again, you say, 'No, I have made up my mind!'

The security guard will not rest, doesn't like change and continues to bombard the administrator, who goes back to the records again for yet more evidence. Finding the security guard is acting in accordance with all things past, the administrator sends the strongest, and most persuasive dopamine-soaked message up to the manager. The spa manager, who has already started to question the decision in the face of such opposition from trusted staff, backs down and allows the administrator to put in an order.

Given this difficult scenario, how can the manager ever make a change? The answer lies in re-educating the security guard and the administrator, updating policy (beliefs) and changing the files held in store (reprioritising memories). In this book, we are updating your beliefs.

When the security guard is given a new brief, and is reassured that all is well, and the administrator is on the side of the manager, the manager can easily and freely make the changes required. Then new records can be established for the future.

Fish and Puppies

IF YOU ARE IN ANY DOUBT about the alcohol con let's look at the analogy of a fish. A fish happily swimming along in a pond sees a bright shiny smaller fish up ahead and is immediately attracted to its prey. The fish sees a little fish as a pleasurable fix for its hunger. What it doesn't know is that the little fish has a sharp hook attached to it. Attracted by the dazzling shimmering reflections of light on the little fish, the big fish swoops on it to then be ensnared by the hook and pulled to land.

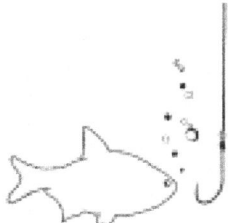

Many fishing waters are for sport only and the fish must be thrown back into the pond or lake. So, the fish has the hook removed, and sometimes it has the line cut if the hook is too difficult to remove, and the fish is thrown back into the water. A day later the fish is swimming along now slightly injured, and sees a small fish, beautifully shiny and bright swimming along in the water in front of it, and it repeats exactly the same process. This continues day after day as the fish becomes more stressed, traumatised, and weaker in the process. Yet every day, unknowingly, fish will still go after the bait. The fish's brain is unable to associate being caught with going after the prey in the first place. It cannot learn. The fish literally flounders and repeats, but now it's swimming around the bottom of the pond trying to get up into the light to find the shiny fish for dinner, in the same way that we sink lower, struggling up to the surface for a gasp of air and some sunlight.

Another analogy is training a puppy. If a puppy does something bad and is reprimanded immediately it will know not to do that thing, but if the reprimand comes five hours after it has done something wrong its brain cannot connect the bad deed with the effect of the punishment.

In the same way our brain is subconsciously unable to associate the physical and psychological aftermath of drinking with taking the drink in the first place. There is a very strong connection between the ability of alcohol to ensnare the drinker, and the length of time it takes the perceived positive effects of alcohol to hit the system of the drinker.

Depending on several factors, alcohol peaks in our system between 10 and 90 minutes after we have first consumed a drink. In the early stages of drinking it takes 30 minutes for us to feel the effect of alcohol on our system, but the anticipatory effect is felt straight away. Just like the Stone Age woman with the coconut, dopamine is released as we reach to get what we think we need. This means that the anticipated effects of alcohol are relatively quick.

Another ingenious aspect to the alcohol con is that the length of time between having your last drink and feeling bad is too long for the subconscious mind to link the two experiences. Just like a puppy being told off five hours after misbehaving, alcohol starts to withdraw from our systems five hours after having our last drink, and our subconscious minds are unable to connect the withdrawal with the act of consuming alcohol. We may know, logically, that our hangover is caused by alcohol, but the learning isn't built into our subconscious mind, and we don't emotionally believe it.

Every day after consuming alcohol we experience the withdrawal symptoms of alcohol, and, for the vast majority of drinkers who fear withdrawal, it is like having a mild flu. The good news is that when the alcohol supply is cut off, with every passing day the feeling of withdrawal is less, and after seven to twelve days all traces of alcohol are out of our system, and our bodies can begin to stabilise.

The con is that alcohol does not relieve stress, it causes it. By now you should be in no doubt about the true nature of alcohol. You are re-educating your subconscious mind by examining the reality of alcohol, and in so doing new beliefs are forming.

Now it is time to build your confidence so that you have self-belief at your side as you outsmart the con artist.

The Fear Con

THE FINAL PART OF THE alcohol confidence trick is highly significant and also ingenious. The final part of the confidence trick is the fear of escape.

In the past, when I was a drinker, I would have said, 'I'm not in denial. I don't have a problem. I enjoy drinking!'

Maybe you've said something similar yourself. We all do!

Denial is a form of fear based on our subconscious mind trying to protect us. When beliefs in our subconscious mind are challenged, the subconscious mind will do everything it can to keep those beliefs true. We will be looking at some of the beliefs around alcohol and unravelling the myths of the con artist in the next section. Fear typically invokes two responses. We either stand and fight, or we run away. The amygdala, or our brain's security guard, triggers the survival response known as the 'fight or flight' response. We can fight by defending ourselves and saying there is no problem, or we can run away by seeking refuge in the very thing that caused the problem in the first place – alcohol. Either way, we stay tied to the con artist by either defending it or running to it for comfort from the nasty people who are ruining our lives and telling us that we have a problem.

Every human being has a fear of change and learning new things. When we are having to unlearn something else first, that fear is even greater. Firstly, it takes courage to admit that we were wrong, and secondly, it takes courage to be open minded and be prepared to learn new things. And that is what is needed here.

Why We Fear Success

Every drinker fears success because when we are trapped we don't think that we can be happy without alcohol in our lives. The alcohol con is truly brilliant because the con artist has made us feel completely reliant.

When we look at a future where we are successful in stopping drinking, we are trying to imagine a future based on what we know now. At the start of this journey our subconscious minds are screaming out that we neither want to, nor can, live a life happily without alcohol in it. And the reason for that is because we imagine our future based on the information that we have at the start, and we are using our imagination to work out the rest.

You are in the process of learning and you have a few more pages yet before you can take that step to the future that you are trying so hard to imagine.

But right now, it is completely understandable that the concept of that future is terrifying, and you fear success.

Every drinker, without exception, feels this fear, so why not feel the fear and step forward anyway.

You may believe that this future state of wonderful, free, and happy sobriety is something that doesn't relate to you. You might think that you're different and it won't work for you. You might think this because you have tried to control, or stop drinking in the past, and it didn't work. Possibly you thought that meant that you had failed.

This feeling of failure does several things – firstly, it reinforces in our mind that to control or stop drinking is an inordinate and mammoth task. People are often so unhappy trying to control alcohol consumption that this reinforces the belief that a future without alcohol is going to be hellish. You would have seen people white knuckling through a dry month challenge, and seen the look of despondency on the faces of designated drivers. This makes it look hard and miserable not to drink! If you have failed in the past to outsmart the con artist, then you can celebrate now, because you are learning a new method, and until now you have been trying to control alcohol with the wrong information, tools and knowledge.

Feeling positive and confident is an important part of the change process, and you have every reason to feel like that now.

Picture yourself on a shore with a lake in front of you. You have had nightmares about that lake being infested with fire-breathing dragons, and you have also been told by other people that there are monsters and fire-breathing dragons in that lake, because the other people have had the same nightmares too. You have seen people step out into the lake and come screaming back in terror, and you have heard tales of hardship and failure. It's a horrible place!

None of these people know how to get across the lake – they are consciously incompetent, frozen in their learning, and without the skills and knowledge that enable them to get across the lake and safely to the other side.

The people on the shore are starving and are plagued with nightmares. They are physically declining, and mentally declining, torn between the nightmares that they have and the knowledge that somewhere on the other side there must be a better way, and there has to be some freedom.

They believe that not only do they have to navigate the lake of monsters and fire-breathing dragons, but they also believe that that when they get to the other side they will still have continuous nightmares. Even worse, they believe that they will also be deprived of the one thing that gives them comfort on their shore of misery – alcohol. Alcohol is the one thing that gives them peace of mind and solace on the hellish shore. How can they possibly survive without it?

What a drinker doesn't realise is that there are no fire-breathing dragons, the lake is a mirage and all they have to do is step through and keep walking. And on the other side there is a land of plenty, with no nightmares, no withdrawal, and no need to control any unfulfilled desires.

On the other side there is no desire to drink, and therefore no torment. The normal stresses of life exist but there is no stress of drinking. On the other shore there is no shame, and no guilt. It was never your fault anyway! On the other shore there is peace of mind. There is self-esteem restored, and there is bountiful health.

The only thing that stands in the way of the journey to the other shore is preparedness to learn to outsmart alcohol by continuing to learn the new skills and acquire the new tools to make the journey. And, like all learning, that requires one thing: an open and enthusuastic mind and preparedness to learn. If you can learn new things in a yoga class, if you can learn in a badminton class or if you can learn in a swimming pool, then you can learn this. You are learning it now.

A fear of the unknown is not an unhealthy fear, and it's a natural biological survival mechanism, but in this scenario the fear of remaining in the present must outweigh the fear of potentially finding total peace. This is the magic button that will help you to change. Any past failures that you've had were not because you're weak, or incapable, or not smart. The failed attempts in the past to stop drinking or to control drinking were purely because of the fact that you did not know that you were in the middle of the ingenious alcohol con, and you didn't have the knowledge, skills or the faith in yourself to get out. You didn't know that everything on the shore is a lie. Do you feel it now? Are you fed up with being on that shore, and are you ready to learn more so that you can walk through the mirage?

I was in the same trap as you for 30 years before I decided that the hell of the shore I was on was somewhere I no longer wanted to live.

Conning Our Basic Human Needs

IN MY WORK AS AN EXECUTIVE coach I worked with clients on variations of a motivational model called Maslow's hierarchy of needs. Maslow developed his theory in the early 1940s, and the hierarchy has a basic premise that one level must be fulfilled before the individual moves on to fulfil the next. During a lifetime we fluctuate between the levels.

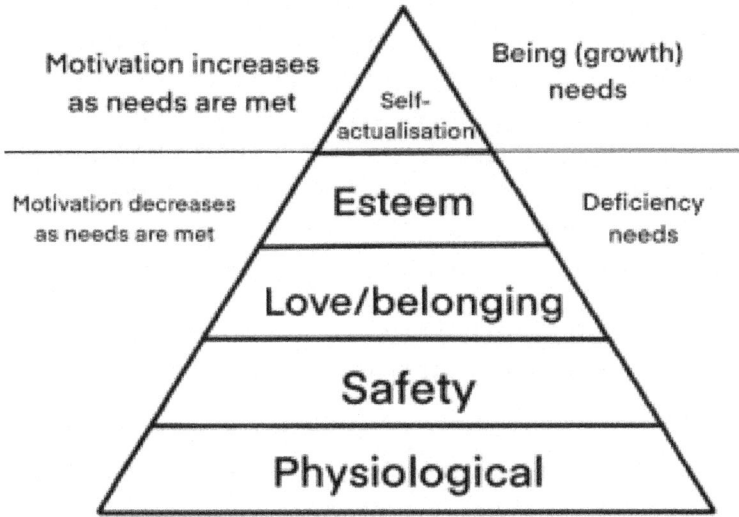

At the very basic level are our survival needs. These needs include food and water, shelter, sleep, sex, and air to breathe. Alcohol attacks our motivation at this very level, and because of its chemical, biological and psychological effects, alcohol is put at this level of need in the subconscious mind.

The alcohol con artist begins to erode our ability to progress up the hierarchy to meet our other more fulfilling needs. Alcohol can damage our safety needs by affecting our health, by affecting our functionality in our jobs, by affecting our basic safety from harm. A woman who is drunk is vulnerable and unable to protect herself. Alcohol affects our ability to function and be accepted in a loving intimate family relationship.

The problems that alcohol causes behind middle-class closed doors is inordinately worse than is ever openly discussed or admitted to. People laugh and joke about their wine o'clock needs, but nobody admits to the damage caused on the other side of alcohol. People don't admit to the role-model damage for the children who watch their parents get drunk every night. There is no openness about the effects of watching a loved one drink to the point of them not being themselves night after night. And be clear here, two glasses of wine are enough for you not to be yourself.

The person who is drunk is never their true authentic self. I want you to be your true, authentic self. That is who you really are.

Every night when we come home from work and we reach for that glass of wine, or the gin and tonic, we're relieving the withdrawal. We are drugging ourselves. People who drink regularly will argue more and say things that they would never say when they're sober, and the effects on our loved ones is far reaching, and deep. The very love and belonging that we require to be happy fulfilled people is being denied us by alcohol. Maslow's hierarchy moves on to our needs for esteem and self-esteem, and alcohol damages our self-esteem in all kinds of ways.

At the top of Maslow's hierarchy of needs is self-actualisation. Self-actualisation is about the desire to become the best person you can be, to give back to others, to be valued and be a valid member of society. The drunk drinker is anything but the self-actualised person that they wish to be, and never the best person they can be.

Life is 24 hours, and it's not just the four or five wine or gin hours that wreck the other 19, by giving us poor degenerative sleep, just to get through the next day for the next fix. And life is more than being grouchy with our loved ones until we do get the next alcohol fix. We are worth far more than that. You are worth more than that.

The alcohol advertising industry understands well our basic human needs. Much of the advertising imagery and messages show alcohol high up the hierarchy of Maslow's triangle. Images portray alcohol as being essential to love and belonging: we see happy, smiling, sophisticated individuals drinking alcohol. That's what the advertising industry wants us to believe.

We don't see the middle-class addict at the bottom of the triangle forced to fulfil their need for a drug like they need water, air or food. That wouldn't sell, would it?

Advertising imagery shows much higher levels of need fulfilment than are the case in practice. The images portray people with high levels of self-esteem, with high confidence happily and sociably consuming the drug. No wonder we think there's something wrong with us when our experience of self-esteem and confidence levels lie shattered in the morning aftermath of drinking the night before. Falling over in the street and arguing with friends and loved ones does nothing to mirror the advertising imagery, which once again is a pure illusion that all drinkers are chasing.

As successful capable well-educated individuals, don't we owe it to ourselves to stop entertaining the con artist and to see through this con?

You are no longer frozen in your learning, because you are reading this book, you are no longer unconsciously incompetent and frozen in the alcohol conundrum. You are now aware that you are an unfortunate victim of an elaborate confidence trick. You are now aware of the addictive nature of alcohol, and its trap.

So, what are you going to do now?

You may still be standing on the burning shore looking out at a lake that you perceived to be full of monsters and fire-breathing dragons, and that's fine. I'm not asking you to step forward yet, but I am asking you to keep an open mind and decide that you are genuinely prepared to keep learning.

Until you opened this book and begun reading the pages you may not have realised that you were standing on that shore with an ever-depleting set of resources as the fires begin to burn. As humans we have an amazing capacity to adapt and be compromised, and because alcohol addiction often happens slowly over many years, we are unaware of its progression. It's only when we raise our head up and start to look around us with fresh perspectives and a fresh set of eyes that we can see that we have got ourselves into a situation that we would not wish upon anybody.

Fear is at best an illusion, and along with the rest of the alcohol illusion that is exactly what fear is in this scenario. It is a feeling, and a very valid one given where you are now, and what you've learned and experienced to date. Having been where you are and felt how you may be feeling I can completely empathise. But remember, we don't know what we don't know, and I am telling you the journey is easy and that the destination is calm, and peaceful and happy.

Playing into the Con Artist's Hands

IF YOU HAVE TRIED IN the past to control how much you drink, you would have used the willpower method. Let's put this one to bed once and for all.

To understand the willpower method let us look to the meaning of will and willpower. Will is the ability to make conscious choice. We all have free will to make our own choices, even if these are to obey the commands of others. Willpower is the motivation to exercise will, and a person with strong willpower will assert decisions even in the face of strong opposition or contradictory indicators. A person with little willpower will give in easily. Getting what you want takes willpower, whether it means you doing something for yourself or others doing something for you. To succeed in anything, this means you must know what you want and then be determined to get it, even in the face of extreme difficulties.

It is interesting to note that people who have tried to stop drinking and failed often consider themselves to be weak when it comes to alcohol, even if they are strong and capable in other areas of their lives, and this adds to the misery caused by alcohol.

It's often the case that it's the strongest willed people who fight hardest both to stop drinking, and to continue drinking. This is because the 'will' in willpower is trying to fight the subconscious mind, which has been programmed to enable you to survive and learnt that alcohol helps you to do that. The subconscious mind is part of our biology and it is flawed, you now know that. Nothing is perfect, and we need to understand that alcohol hijacks our natural biology. Our subconscious minds are programmed by the psychology of addiction to believe that having a drink is exactly what we need to help us relieve stress and help us get pleasure. And so, the more stressed that we feel about drinking, the more our subconscious mind will tell us to have a drink to solve our problems. Although the subconscious mind believes it is helping, it is doing the opposite.

The 'battle of wills' between two people is a well understood situation that involves people who try to defeat each other by refusing to change their mind, and hoping their opponent will weaken first. Remember, the conscious mind is 5% of our mind, and the subconscious powerhouse is 95%.

In a battle of the conscious mind versus subconscious mind where the subconscious mind is permanently awake, permanently on guard, and permanently ready to meet our every need, the 5% conscious mind is, in the long term, no adversary for the subconscious will.

A group for mothers watching their toddlers play in a nursery will talk about how strong-willed their two-year-old is, and how tormenting and exhausting it is to fight them. A two-year-old child will do everything they can to exert their authority and get what they want from their parents. The parents who give in to these tantrums are the ones that continue to have problems for many years to come, as the child realises that her screams and shouts made her parents weaken and give in.

When it comes to the alcohol conundrum the toddler is your subconscious mind. The parent who understands that the shouting, stamping and demanding behaviour is the response of a threatened and helpless child, is a firm parent, who is calm and clear about what they want, and educates the child that their behaviour and demands are unacceptable. Battling against a will head-to-head is exhausting.

Willpower is finite and it runs out. Much like a battery its energy will deplete. If you have used some willpower in a busy meeting during the day to get your point across, or if you've used willpower to go for a run in the morning that you were in two minds whether to go on, there may not be any willpower left to argue with your enormous subconscious about not having a drink.

The battle of the wills that ensues when trying to control alcohol using the willpower method is doomed to failure. You know that this cognitive dissonance or mental battle is exhausting. Remember, the body always seeks balance, or homoeostasis, and when it comes to a mental battle eventually the decision-making part of our minds backs down to restore equilibrium.

Until the subconscious childlike mind is faced with re-learning what it understands to be helpful in relation to alcohol, then its strength will always win over the conscious 5% of our minds. The subconscious mind is very powerful in many ways. We are here now educating our childlike subconscious - we are beginning to parent our subconscious mind.

Many people mistakenly try to control their subconscious minds by constantly forcing themselves to cut down or stop drinking only to find themselves failing. The way to end the cognitive dissonance, and the mental battle that rages between the conscious and the subconscious mind is to re-educate the subconscious mind, so that there is one mind wanting one thing.

That is what the clients at The Alcohol Coach do every day using the methods and blueprints developed.

The subconscious mind is like a little child that acts on its desires and emotions while ignoring everything else. It wants the things that it wants right away, without waiting and with disregard to any social norms. The subconscious mind is very powerful, and it cares for nothing except getting what it thinks your body needs to survive, and this can lead to serious problems.

It may sound very strange when you understand that despite the subconscious mind being an amazing powerhouse for your body and your survival, it's also open to misinterpreting and misunderstanding what it sees and what it learns. It's susceptible to being conned.

This is particularly true in the case of our relationship with alcohol. Our subconscious mind interprets the relief of getting a drink as being of benefit. Because we feel the relief of consuming alcohol, we conclude that it's beneficial. The subconscious mind does not understand that the relief it's experiencing is not true pleasure but is partially relieving the void and the anxiety that the previous drink caused.

This is why your determined, conscious mind, that you have relied on in so many other aspects of your life, has failed you until now in its latest challenge to control alcohol. You will be excused for feeling like you have failed and that you weren't strong enough. The fact is you are completely strong enough, and you are stronger than you even know, because it is your own subconscious mind that is working very hard and winning at convincing you that you must have a drink.

It is the same subconscious mind that drives you to success in other areas because it has learnt over the years that you are capable of success, and of fulfilling your goals.

When that familiar feeling of withdrawal hits, the subconscious mind comes up with the answer to make you feel better – have alcohol. And once your subconscious mind is on the path of getting you that drink it will not rest until it wins. As a strong minded and strong-willed individual, the very thing that causes you success in other areas is causing your downfall here.

The solution is very easy, both in theory and, as you will realise, in practice. The solution is simply to re-educate your subconscious mind so that it works with your conscious thoughts, your determination and courage, and not against it. Your subconscious mind is changing as you read these words. It is no longer so sure about how helpful alcohol is to you. It has begun accepting that is was misled in the past.

One of the most well-known sources of support for alcohol is Alcoholics Anonymous. This organisation formed by Bill Wilson in 1935 has been responsible for saving the lives of hundreds of thousands of people, and its philosophy has changed little since it was founded. When I was concerned about my drinking pattern, I thought that the AA was the only place to go for advice, and one day I rang.

On the other end of the phone was a lovely man called John, and I spent about 10 minutes on the phone to John which ended up with me coaching him. I opened the conversation by asking him for some advice as to whether he thought I may be an alcoholic or not, and it transpired that John had not had alcohol for many years and that he'd lived one day at a time, resisting alcohol, and the temptation to drink.

I was appalled that somebody should have to live their life in such a state of torment and fear that their resoluteness would fail them. The reasons that AA stops people drinking is not just to do with the exercising of willpower but it's to do with various other things such as admitting to be completely helpless in the face of addiction, to admit to being an alcoholic and to hand over the whole situation to a higher power.

None of that fitted well with me. I've never been helpless, I don't think the term 'alcoholic' is helpful, and there is no way I was going to hand my life over to a higher power.

On all accounts the AA was of no interest to me whatsoever.

The AA is an organisation that helps many people, but I did not want to I put myself through its methods or ideology. It went completely against my concept of living a free and independent life, so I decided to look elsewhere for the help that I felt I needed to get out of the trap.

The process led me to use my own resources, and through my science degree, and masters level coaching I started asking a different set of questions and went on to research involving hundreds of books and medical papers. Since unravelling the alcohol addiction conundrum, I have also added addiction training, life coaching and other therapies to my tool kit. This book brings much of this learning together.

Meaningless Words

THERE ARE MANY TERMS used in relation to alcohol that for most drinkers are unhelpful and damaging.

The most significant is the word 'alcoholic'. The word alcoholic labels a person, and once labelled, they carry it for life. The word alcoholic conjures up an image of somebody who has hit rock bottom, or is homeless and lost everything and continues to drink on a continuous basis and is on the verge of death. This label is unhelpful and inaccurate. It's unhelpful because it is the only question that drinkers use as a yardstick for whether they have a problem that they need to address. It goes something like this ...

'Am I an alcoholic?'

'No.'

'That's okay then.'

There is no room in that definition for any of the *problem drinkers* I've ever met and ever known.

You may have heard that alcoholism is a disease and that it is a disease for which there is no cure. That is a very worrying and inaccurate definition. It's worrying because the very existence of the definition is stopping millions of people realising that they do have an alcohol problem, and that they are addicted to alcohol.

And what about the issue of it being an incurable disease? Our human brain is highly adaptive, and we unlearn and learn new things all the time.

Once the con trick that is alcohol is unravelled, our subconscious mind would have learnt new ways of thinking about alcohol. It is in these new ways of thinking that lies freedom, and these new ways of thinking are in no way connected to any kind of incurable disease.

When I was concerned about my drinking, I went to my local physician and asked her if she thought I was an alcoholic. She asked me many questions including:

'Do I drink first thing in the morning?' to which I said, 'No,' and her conclusion was that it was up to me to decide if I was an alcoholic or not.

It wasn't the doctor's fault that she was trying to diagnose a disease that could not be diagnosed. There is no blood test, there is no brain scan, there is no X-ray that can diagnose alcoholism. In fact, there is no test at all.

The problem with the terms alcoholic and alcoholism is that millions of capable, successful people who are suffering from alcohol addiction will continue to suffer until it is recognised that there is a pandemic of people who are addicted to alcohol.

It's ironic that some schools of thought purport to the fact that alcoholism is incurable, and people are kept in purgatory for the rest of their lives trying to resist, and fearing what will happen to them if they don't resist alcohol. If it were incurable, then people would not be escaping the trap using the method that I am giving you here in this book.

People are walking away from the trap without looking back with no need for willpower, with no mental torture, and no desire to ever drink again. That is not a criterion of any incurable disease. Because if it were then it starts to sound like witchcraft or magic which it most certainly is not.

The problem with addiction is largely psychological. The problem with addiction lies in the subconscious mind, and the way out lies in working with the subconscious mind.

In addition to getting in touch with AA and going to see my doctor I also went to see a counsellor to ask about my drinking patterns, and whether or not I might be an alcoholic. The counsellor started asking me a series of questions one of which also included the 'Do you drink first thing in the morning?' question. When I said no, she said I wasn't an alcoholic and she started to explore with me the reasons why I drank alcohol.

Most of us have some issues related to our pasts, whether minor or major, and rooting around you are bound to find something.

We may be anxious socially, or we may feel that we can't lose weight when we should be able to, or we may have issues forming deep relationships, or issues over going outside, or being indoors, or any number of a million different things that affect all of us to a certain extent. A counsellor will focus on these issues as a reason for somebody drinking, but they are completely misunderstanding the whole process of addiction. It is almost as though counsellors don't realise alcohol is an addictive substance, so by asking 'Why am I drinking?' 'What are the underpinning reasons for my drinking?' is irrelevant.

The reason that I drank alcohol is the same reason that all drinkers drink alcohol, and that is to get the alcohol. I drank because I was addicted to alcohol.

That may have been beautifully packaged in subconscious phrases that told me it was relaxing me, or I needed it because I was stressed, or I was feeling in a really good mood so I needed to celebrate, or I had an argument with my partner, or I was feeling really frustrated. But that's what it was: it was well-packaged self-talk. The reason I drank was to get my fix of alcohol, which is exactly the same reason every drinker drinks.

The counsellor asked me about the reasons why I drink, the doctor asked me to decide myself if I had the disease called alcoholism, and John at the AA told me that he spent every single day of his life trying to avoid having a drink. After consulting three experts about a problem I was trying to find out if I had, I drew a complete blank.

It was therefore clear to me that neither the organisation that is deemed to be head of knowledge for alcohol, nor the medical profession, nor the counselling profession had anything to offer me. It was through my executive coaching work and science degree that I uncovered the solution by starting to ask a different set of questions.

The fact is that people drink because they are addicted to a drug; that drug is alcohol and it is highly addictive. That is the only reason people drink. People have trauma: some people suffer from anxiety and some people are thrill seekers. That does not mean that they will become addicted to alcohol, it just means that they need ways to manage their thoughts and emotions in healthy ways so that their needs are met.

When my mother was pregnant with me, she was told by her doctor that if she wanted a small baby that would be less painful to deliver, she should smoke because smoking will reduce the size of a baby at birth and will be less painful. This was genuine advice given out by doctors in those days, with the information that they had at the time. We now know that nicotine is a highly addictive drug and lung cancer caused by smoking accounts for more deaths than any other type of cancer.

Alcohol causes more deaths than all illicit drugs combined. Even with this knowledge the general public still tends to believe that alcohol is an acceptable form of relaxation. Science tells us something different.

Some drinkers fear that alcohol addiction is genetic or hereditary. Sixty years ago, 80% of British men smoked cigarettes and in 2020 that figure was 16%. If addiction is genetic that means that entire genetic makeup of a nation has changed in just 60 years. Isn't it more likely that through education, awareness and changing beliefs that less people are becoming addicted to nicotine because less people are getting involved with the drug in the first place, and that more people have escaped the nicotine smoking trap?

People would generally agree that there are either smokers or non-smokers, and that anybody who smokes, regardless of how much, is a smoker. They are addicted to nicotine and they are a smoker. There is no term for somebody who smokes 60 or 80 cigarettes a day compared to ten, and they certainly wouldn't be told that they are smokeaholics suffering from a lifelong disease called smokeaholism, for which there is no cure.

Most people know of somebody who has stopped smoking and is happily a non-smoker. If you know other people who have stopped using the willpower method then you will be experiencing them caught in the insufferable position of always wanting something that they can't have.

I found myself in a family situation recently where I declined an alcoholic drink and ordered something non-alcoholic. One of my family members smiled and asked me if I wasn't drinking because I was an alcoholic. I resisted the temptation to laugh out loud and swallowed a smile to myself as I looked at the absolute irony of the situation.

If I had declined a shot of heroin do you think I would have been asked if I was a heroin addict because it wasn't something I wanted, or if I refused a cigarette would I be asked if I was a nicotine addict because I refused a cigarette? No, I wouldn't.

Alcohol is the only drug that you have to justify not taking, and it's the only drug that people will think you're addicted to if you're not consuming it. It's the people who take it who are addicted, or the people who struggle not to want it. When you don't want an addictive drug, you are free.

People still believe that someone who has stopped drinking is an alcoholic, and that they will continue to be alcoholics until the day they die, struggling in recovery.

When you understand the truth there is absolutely nothing to recover from other than getting your whole self back in alignment and becoming fulfilled in ways that you currently cannot imagine. If there are smokers and non-smokers, then there are drinkers and non-drinkers.

The solution to alcohol addiction, although multifaceted, is really very simple for the vast majority: open your mind, explore the evidence, challenge your beliefs of the benefits, learn some facts, gain some skills, and walk to freedom. This is what I teach at The Alcohol Coach.

The development of an addiction to alcohol can take many years or decades to go from occasional consumption to a serious problem, or it can happen over a series of months. There are many factors that affect the rapidity of the entry into the alcohol trap. It is often the more educated, successful and sociable people who drink more, drink faster, and sink most quickly into the trap.

There are many reasons for this. People who are better educated tend to drink heavily at College or University and so the reward mechanisms and pathways and learning in the subconscious are well established at a relatively young age. This group of people also then tend to go on to get more high-powered jobs, and high achievers are often encouraged to drink after work, and they are also likely to suffer from more stress-related conditions connected with work.

The work hard, play hard ethic is strong and so successful people often drink a lot. Women, in particular, are falling into the alcohol trap in droves. When women pause or stop their careers to have children, they can quickly fall into the end-of-day stress-relieving category of problem drinkers. Wine o'clock is anything but fine o'clock, and hundreds of thousands of women at home with children are drinking with the perceived benefits of giving them some kind of enjoyable freedom at the end of the day, or relaxing because they've had a hard day looking after the children. Once the addiction is established it tends to grow over time, with a sneaky glass at lunchtime, or a bottle while cooking the dinner, and then even when the children have left home, it carries on.

Better educated and successful people have a higher disposable income which means that when it comes to financing alcohol addiction there are no barriers, and expensive wines and the best gins find their way into the booze cupboard at home.

The amount of alcohol drunk is also influenced by childhood and the role modelling of parents, parents' friends and the group and social life of a child when growing up. A child brought up in an environment where the parents are seen to have parties, to entertain, and where alcohol is free-flowing, is likely to associate the perceived benefits with alcohol more strongly and from a younger age, which means that these people are likely to fall into the trap more quickly and more heavily than people who were brought up without these influences.

There is an interesting issue here around family influences. It was thought that there were addictive personalities and that alcohol consumption was somehow genetic. The reasons are much more likely due to the subconscious learning of the child growing up in a household where she learns from the role modelling of her parents that this is what is expected.

The addictive personality idea is also reinforced by the fact that people who take one drug will take another. In reality, people who take drugs tend to stick together, so smokers will stick together with smokers, and they are also likely to drink as well. It is very rare that you will find people who don't drink who smoke, it is more normal that people started smoking and then drinking was part of that process.

When people drink, their inhibitions are lowered and their control centre is diminished which means that they are likely to smoke a lot more when they are drunk, and even if they rarely smoke, they may find themselves smoking when they are drunk.

Using the idea of an addictive personality is a form of denial, and an excuse for not taking responsibility for the problem.

There has been a link discovered between addiction and people who suffer from anxiety, and also people who seek excitement, and these dispositions may be genetic. But there are many more productive and healthy ways to address anxiety, and live a life that is more exciting than hurling headlong into a bottle of oblivion. The more alcohol we drink, the less resilient we become and the less fun our lives are. Once away from the con artist we can start to build resilience and coping mechanisms and thrive in new and exciting ways.

Casual and Controlled Drinkers

THE PROGRESS OF OUR alcohol addiction can take years, or decades, and sometimes it hovers on the edge for a lifetime. This does not mean that so-called 'casual drinkers' are not addicted. To a certain extent they are, and alcohol will be affecting their health in ways they may never understand. It can be tempting to look at this group of drinkers with envy but in fact they are still taking a highly addictive and dangerous drug, and they are still at risk of serious health issues and becoming more addicted.

There are many phrases that are used around alcohol when drinkers are asked why they drink, and I've used them myself. I used to say things like 'I can take it or leave it', or 'It's not doing me any harm'. When you look at these statements, they are usually negative. They are not positive reasons to do something.

Society and the media have built up the consumption of alcohol as a treat that we give ourselves because we have earnt it. Would having a spoonful of arsenic be seen as a treat? Alcohol is a highly toxic, cancer-causing drug and is anything but a treat.

If alcohol is so amazing and so enjoyable, why is a whole industry built around people taking mini breaks from it? Dry challenges are common, and taking a break from alcohol is a good idea, but think about it ... you now know that anybody who needs to prove that they can control something clearly has a problem.

When we start drinking again after a dry challenge, we often find that very quickly we are back to the levels of consumption we were at before, or are drinking even more. The nature of addiction is to drink more over time because we are naturally driven and motivated to get our survival motivation hormone, dopamine.

For a casual drinker to remain as a casual drinker, two things need to happen: firstly, they need to be unmotivated to seek more alcohol over time as the dopamine reward gets less. Remember the stone age woman and the coconut? The dopamine reward gets less for doing the same thing, so we are motivated to work harder for the reward. When you look back on how much you were drinking 10 or 15 years ago, is it more now?

Work is needed to take a drug and maintain a status quo of consumption, and for a casual drinker to stay a casual drinker that takes effort.

You will know people who can have a single glass of wine from a bottle and put it back without a flicker, while you're sitting there thinking, 'How did you do that? Why did you do that? Don't you want the rest?'

There are people who don't drink for emotional reasons like fun, or stress. Addiction hasn't developed because the pathways in their brain haven't made the connections or established the beliefs strongly. But this doesn't mean that these connections won't develop, and there is always a risk. If a disaster or significant life-change befell the person, they are likely to believe that alcohol will make them feel better, because that is their lifelong experience of watching the rest of society.

Lots of so-called casual drinkers are addicted to alcohol and are on the treadmill trying to moderate or cut down what they drink, and, for many, alcohol will be causing them stress and misery.

Cutting Down

WHEN WE FIRST REALISE that we have a problem, the first thing that we are likely to do is to try to cut down the amount we drink. It may be a desire to cut down that bought you to this book.

In order to cut down, we will need to be conscious of what we are drinking in a way we weren't previously. We will need to think about alcohol more and will need to exercise control in the form of willpower. So, we start to make rules for ourselves.

We'll decide not to drink at certain times or on certain days, or we'll make rules for ourselves to only have two or three drinks instead of four or five that we normally have. Rather than finishing the second bottle, we won't open it, or we'll open the first bottle and only drink half. We'll start marking the bottle with a marker pen so that we don't go past it. All of these things may work for some time, but will never last because we are working against our natural survival instincts (that alcohol has hijacked) and we are just changing our behaviour and not our underlying thinking, beliefs or desires.

Once we've followed our self-imposed rules for a while, we'll convince ourselves that we don't have a problem anymore, or we'll decide our rules were pointless, or maybe we'll just give up.

Something will spark an emotional reaction, or there will be a special occasion, or reason to have a blow out and all of our intentions are forgotten. It takes hard work to cut down or moderate.

Many of us will start a new exercise regime with high levels of determination and willpower, and we'll do it religiously for a couple of weeks until something throws us off course.

When our willpower and determination to control what we drink fades, the psychological relief of having a drink will be so great that the subconscious will once again interpret alcohol as being really good for us, and the addiction will be stronger than previously.

The subconscious mind, whilst it is left unchecked around its perceived benefits of alcohol, will do everything in its power to give you the drink it thinks you want and need. So even if you have decided that you want to cut down, or you want to stop, your subconscious mind will be working hard in the background. Your child-like subconscious mind is doing its best.

The well intentioned subconscious mind will be telling your conscious mind that 'just one won't hurt' or 'we deserve it because we've had a particularly trying day,' or 'we deserve it because the children are being particularly annoying,' or because our spouse has said something particularly unpleasant to us. The reality is that until the subconscious mind is re-educated the problem will prevail, and it will get worse.

Alcohol destroys the health of everyone who drinks, in the same way that smoking does. Alcohol also eats away at wealth; it destroys relationships and destroys our wellbeing.

When we try to control alcohol and fail, we find it confusing and alarming: we start to panic. Like the fish on the line, we realise that we're hooked. A person who is strong-willed, capable, successful and motivated in many areas of his or her life becomes defeated in the face of increasing alcohol consumption, the strong will fades, and confidence and self-esteem also fade to be replaced by guilt, shame and inadequacy.

We start to wonder what is wrong with us and why we can't control this aspect of our lives when we're capable of controlling other aspects. This leads to confusion, uncertainty and stress, and leads to us reaching for the one thing that we know will relieve the stress – alcohol.

Even drinkers who think they're in control and who abstain from alcohol for a few weeks and months are addicted to alcohol.

So, what prompts one drinker to attempt to cut down and another to continue unheeded? It all depends on where the drinker is in the trap, and how aware they are.

The fish attracted to the bright shiny lure is oblivious to the dangers that lie ahead, until it realises that it's hooked. Up until that point the fish is happy and fearless, and it will happily pursue its goal. At the point that it realises it's trapped it will start to panic, struggle and resist entrapment. For us as drinkers, this is the point where we start to try to control how much and when we drink. Remember the learning stages. At this stage we are unfrozen. We start to flounder.

We soon realise that it's not that easy, and whereas we didn't know we had a problem before, we do now. Whereas before, we were unconsciously incompetent and frozen in our knowledge, we're not any longer. Now we are floundering because it isn't as easy to stop as we thought.

At this point just like the fish we start to panic and struggle, and as we feel more stressed and caught, we will drink more.

We continue to drink and progress from drinking because we think we enjoy it, to drinking to alleviate negative feelings, a growing number of which come from drinking itself.

Fun ⟶ Relief from stress, boredom, loneliness, frustration ⟶ **Misery**

Our subconscious mind is learning throughout the process of addiction because the chemical and neurological reaction to the drug is inadvertently teaching it. We have no control over this, until we decide to re-educate ourselves with the truth, and outsmart the con.

The progression of alcohol addiction from something we did for fun to full blown misery is slow and subtle.

Alcohol fills our emotional gaps like pouring a jug of water over a surface with holes in it. Eventually every emotion that we have will trigger a response to reach for a drink, and that is because our subconscious mind has been taught that alcohol is what's needed.

If we've been drinking unknowingly to alleviate anxiety, stress, depression, sadness, loneliness, boredom or frustration for a number of years, then the pathways in our brain for doing this are learned and strong and established. The more repetition there is, the more learning, and that leads to more neural connections between alcohol and different emotions.

But, in addition to that, we've stopped growing and using our own resources to meet our emotional needs. We can learn to meet our emotional needs in more resilient and healthy ways once we have broken free from alcohol.

When we realise that we are unable to control how much we drink, whether it's on a daily basis or binge drinking, it starts to seriously undermine our confidence.

All so-called casual drinkers are on this path, and people who cut down or try to control what they drink are too.

When a Smart Person Feels Stupid

WHEN A STRONG-MINDED, capable person is unable to accomplish something that they think ought to be straightforward, like cutting down on the amount of alcohol consumed, or stopping completely, the effect on levels of confidence is significant.

We start asking ourselves 'What's wrong with me? Why can't I control myself around alcohol?' This is made worse by the outdated perceptions in society and the media where it is considered that people who are unable to control the level of alcohol consumption are weak, pathetic, and out of control.

This may be the stereotypical image of the alcoholic who has lost everything, but, more and more it's becoming a commonplace cause of family arguments and grief behind closed doors.

The good news is that when we realise that we have been victims of a clever con trick, and we start learning, we can get our power back and we can outsmart it.

Let's recap on how the con started and how the cycle of reward and withdrawal began.

The first drink we ever had made us feel sick and dizzy and we probably didn't like it, but we'd met the con artist and the trap had been sprung.

At this point we may have vowed never to have another drink, but the benefits of alcohol had been sold to us all our lives by family and friends who were also being conned. Our beliefs were established in our subconscious mind based on what we had seen and heard, and how we experienced the effects of alcohol. This led to assumptions and incorrect interpretations.

Beliefs

↓

Conclusions

↓

Assumptions and Interpretations

↓

Experience/ Observations

Beliefs were established in our subconscious minds along with the tooth fairy and Santa Claus. We concluded that alcohol didn't harm us, and it didn't really do very much for us, but we wanted this amazing thing that we'd been told about and seen others with. We believed what we'd been told, and we believed what we'd been sold. So, we tried another drink.

In this book, we are bringing the old and long-established beliefs up to the surface of our minds, like bubbles in a lemonade bottle, we are challenging them, and popping the bubbles, so that new conclusions can be drawn and new beliefs formed.

At no point did we decide we wanted to become addicted to alcohol, and there was never a point when we noticed it happening, because the con was working on our subconscious mind and that's where the solution lies.

The Con Artist's Stories

AS SOMEBODY WHO HAS been a victim of the alcohol con myself, I fell hook, line and sinker for all the con artists stories. My ever eager-to-please subconscious mind was oblivious to the truth beneath the lies. There are two essential aspects to the con artist's story in terms of why we drink, and they relate to the idea of expectancy.

Addictive beliefs can be thought of as a cluster of ideas that we have centred around pleasure-seeking, and relief and escape. It will surprise you to learn that the list of beliefs below are true of all drug addicts, regardless of the drug. You may see yourself in the beliefs below, and they are true for cocaine addicts, alcohol addicts, nicotine addicts, and heroin addicts. The fact that alcohol is completely socially acceptable, and that it's okay to voice these ideas in public and to share the symptoms of addiction with friends and family is bizarre. Yet we do. We openly state that we need a drink, and can't wait to relax at wine o'clock, or that it's so boring we're going to down a few beers, or when we're feeling low that we deserved a treat (of poison!).

The people we're talking to are also oblivious of drug addiction, so they use the same language, not knowing that they are talking about drug addiction. See if you recognise yourself in any of these symptoms of drug addiction:

1. The belief that the drug will bring us calm.

2. The expectation that the drug will improve our social ability and enjoyment.

3. The expectation that we will find pleasure and excitement.

4. The belief that the drug will energise us.

5. The expectation that the drug will have a soothing effect.

6. The assumption that the drug will relieve boredom, anxiety, tension and depression.

7. The conviction that unless something is done to satisfy the craving, or to neutralise the distress, it will continue indefinitely and possibly get worse.

In addition to these expectations and beliefs, drug addicts have a variety of beliefs relevant to firstly, justifying why it's okay to do it, and secondly, rationalising why they're entitled to do it. For example, we may find ourselves saying:

'Since I'm feeling bad it's okay for me to have a drink,' and in this way we *justify* having alcohol, or we may say,

'I've been working really hard, therefore I deserve a drink,' because we feel *entitled*.

It was only when I started to analyse the alcohol confidence trick that I looked at the way alcohol had conned me into believing that it was doing more and more for me. The different things that I believed alcohol did for me I realised were split into two main areas

1. The belief that alcohol added good stuff to my life (anticipatory).

2. The belief that alcohol took away bad stuff from my life (relief).

You will not be alone in thinking the alcohol makes you and social situations more fun. My clients at The Alcohol Coach are all concerned initially about how solving their alcohol problem will impact on their social life, but the outcome is that they are thriving and more vibrant without alcohol in their lives.

You are amongst millions in believing that alcohol injects enjoyment into your life, and every evening around the country many thousands of people reach for a bottle of toxic drug to alleviate stress from a busy or difficult day.

The nature of the alcohol con is that it will offer you anything you believe it will offer you, whilst giving you nothing but misery.

The brilliant news is that all you need to do is unravel the con artist's stories and see through the clever lies, and you will find it easy and joyful to walk away with your head held high, a spring in your step and a victorious smile.

A con artist can only con you when they have the upper hand, but with every sentence that you read and truth that you uncover you will have nothing but disrespect and disgust for the confidence trickster that is alcohol.

Let's unravel some of the con artist's stories.

The con artists' stories are the benefits that we have been led to believe as being truths about alcohol. Some of these we have learned from family, friends and society from a very young age, some from advertising and the media, and others from our own physical experience of dopamine learning pathways being hijacked, and feelings of stress relief. In this section we explore and challenge each so-called benefit. When you look very closely, with an open and challenging mind you will see that it is all a con, and an illusion. The stories and supposed beliefs are discussed in two parts: the believed benefits around anticipation and fun, and the believed benefit around bringing relief and helping us.

Con Artist Stories around Anticipation: Alcohol is Fun!

Alcohol is Fun: I Enjoy Drinking

We will be excused from initially thinking that consuming alcohol is fun and therefore making it a self-fulfilling prophecy that drinking is enjoyable. The long con has been operating since the minute we were born in every avenue of our lives, in the media, in entertainment, in our role models, and in our family and friends.

If you have been in a social situation in the past and not been able to drink because you were the designated driver, and you wanted to drink, that's not fun.

When you want something, and you can't have it you will feel miserable.

You might think that having alcohol would make you happy, but in truth it's only not having it that makes you unhappy. Having alcohol doesn't make you happy, it makes you feel the relief of getting it.

If it were so enjoyable then the memories and the times spent drinking would be highly focused on the drink itself.

If you think back to a wonderful day in your life, perhaps a beautiful drive out to the countryside, or a vibrant day in a city, the birth of a child, or marriage, the images captured in your mind will be vibrant, there will be people, beautiful scenes and maybe a stunning storm or sunshine.

133

These are the photographic memories of your life and the other things that we remember. I don't remember vividly any single individual glass of wine.

The glass that promised freedom was a trap.

This is why the confidence trick works so well, and why millions of people fall into the trap every year. There is no freedom in a glass of poison. How could there possibly be? There is no frivolity in sitting at home on the sofa thinking you're having fun drinking a bottle of wine alone. As your brain shuts down, your eyesight fades and your senses dim, and as the poison takes hold. That is not enjoyment.

When life as a drinker is enjoyable it is enjoyable despite alcohol and not because of it. Life is enjoyable because of the friends you meet, the places you go to, and the things that you do. When life is enjoyable you feel it with every sense functioning brightly, healthily and boldly.

Life is 24 hours and not four or five hours in a night, and it is certainly not the 30 minutes or an hour in a drinking session when the withdrawal is relieved, and you feel a slight buzz. That is not your life. That is not fun!

The slight buzz after the relief is short-lived, and is followed by a surge of stress hormones in your body that then needs to be dampened down by the next drink. Relief is not fun!

If you're out for an evening with friends, so what if they are in the cycle of withdrawal, relief, and slight buzz? Is that really enjoyable? Is it enjoyable to wake up with a hangover and remorse? Is it enjoyable to be short tempered and irritable?

What exactly is enjoyable about taking off a tight pair of shoes? Enjoyment isn't relief when the thing that caused the stress didn't need to happen in the first place. Surely, it's more fun to not live in a state where relief is needed, but in one that is happy, calm and content all the time.

If drinking is so much fun, why do so many social situations deteriorate into chaos? Just go to any town after midnight and watch all the fights and arguments breaking out as people stagger down the street. Just watch a social group at a dinner party when people start getting loud and obnoxious or overly sensitive and offensive. Try being a fly on the wall back home after the social event is over, and watch the arguments and insults fly between two people who would never behave like that sober. This is the reality. Look at this closely, and you will understand it for what it is.

Everybody knows what is meant by 'a con', but what it refers to is something malicious that we have taken into our confidence and something we have trusted to be true. The best enjoyments to be had in the alcohol confidence trick are to outsmart the con artist and to get out with exhilaration and pride.

Alcohol is Fun: I am No Longer Bored

Do you drink alcohol to alleviate boredom? Many people do.

It's true that time passes more quickly after drinking a bottle or two of wine, but then again time passes quickly when you sleep for a few hours. If you just want time to go with no activity in it, why not just go to sleep?

A person who is not bored is a person who is active physically or mentally. A person who is not bored is creative. A person who is not bored is doing something.

I know that it can sometimes be difficult to motivate ourselves to do something, especially in the evenings when we're tired. But if we have had a full and active day, and are not being dragged down by alcohol, then feeling a little weary is okay. It's normal. Eat some food, relax with a favourite show, or take a walk. Use this time for self care.

When we drink regularly, we are permanently stressed and anxious until we receive our next fix of alcohol. We feel agitated.

The agitation is caused by the slight physical craving due to the withdrawal effects of the previous drink, and because of the subconscious thoughts in which we've wrongly concluded that relieving the withdrawal of alcohol is a pleasure.

The relief of something unpleasant can only ever be a relief. It can never be a pleasure. It's like saying that the annoying car alarm is pleasurable when it stops. It's the relief of the car alarm stopping which is perceived as being pleasurable.

Being glad that something has stopped isn't entertaining.

Drinking for boredom just means that you're drunk and bored, because you're still not doing anything. You are not being creative, truly relaxing or giving anything positive to yourself. Slowly numbing your senses only to wake tomorrow feeling awful is very boring indeed.

Alcohol is Fun: It Helps at Social Events

One thing that I realised about myself after I stopped drinking is that I have a slight social anxiety issue. This issue had been camouflaged by drink my whole life. If I was going out for the evening and I felt anxious, I'd pour myself a glass of wine while I was getting ready to go out. And when I got out, I'd get my hands on a drink as soon as I could. After two glasses of wine my inhibitions were gone, and I was the life and soul of the party... I had arrived!

There were two problems with this. Firstly, my social anxiety, although slightly unpleasant, was there for a reason, I'm an introvert, I can feel a bit awkward, and I care about what people think.

What alcohol did was to take away my natural inhibitions so that I became bolder and more courageous in social situations. The problem was that I often embarrassed myself, and I said things and did things that I wouldn't normally have wanted to do.

And so the people I socialised with never got to know the true me, the quieter version, the person who preferred listening to them rather than forcing her point of view on them. And the second problem is that my mild social anxiety was camouflaged for 30 years and so was never dealt with. It is only now that I am becoming braver and dealing with social situations properly. Because I'm not drinking I'm also calmer going into social situations, which may seem ironic, but it is true. Once other people have started drinking, and after a couple of glasses of wine, which will normally take most people 30 minutes into an evening, no one really notices whether I've got a drink or not. I find it easy to relax and laugh and be silly if I want to because nobody is watching and everybody else is too drunk to care anyway.

The additional benefits are that I wake up in the morning without a hangover. You will notice that after a few hours with other people drinking, the conversation starts to deteriorate to nonsense, people get boring, or obnoxious, and they tend to laugh less. And by then, the party really has peaked. Why not take the best of it, and go home?

Do you think of yourself as the life and soul of the party? I did. For 30 years I was the life and soul of the party with a glass in my hand. The irony is, that every single person I have met who now wishes they could control their alcohol consumption, also says that they are the life and soul of the party. How can we all be the life and soul of the party? Is it more the truth we're all behaving like drugged idiots?

Alcohol is a mild stimulant and a strong depressive. For every laugh you may think it gives you it takes away two or maybe even ten.

If you're reading this, it's because alcohol has made you miserable and you want to change that. Now you're beginning to see through the con trick that you and millions of others fall for, you're about to make that change and enjoy life so much more.

Alcohol is Fun: It Brightens My Night when I'm Stuck at Home with the Kids

Having been a single mother for the best part of 10 years, believe me, I can empathise with needing to brighten up an evening when you're home alone with children asleep upstairs and you are unable to go out. What would you think if somebody told you that injecting heroin brightened up the night? Do you really think that taking an addictive drug that poisons your system, destroys your self-esteem and confidence, ages you, and makes you less able to cope with life is really brightening up your night? I think you know the answer.

The relief of fulfilling a perceived need is what you think is brightening up your night, but this is an illusion, because alcohol takes away the brightness not just that evening, but the next morning as well.

We are here to outsmart the con artist, and once you have lost confidence in the con artist you will never trust or believe in it again, and everything it made you believe you will know is untrue.

All that then remains is for you to have some tools and techniques to outsmart it completely and rid yourself of this truly malicious con artist for good.

Alcohol is Fun: It Wakes Me Up when I'm Tired

I used to think that drinking in the evening had a positive influence on my energy levels, because by the time I had done a day's work, cooked a meal and looked after children I was exhausted.

The bottle or two of wine in the evening woke me up and gave me a new burst of energy. This was particularly true at the weekend if I was going out and felt too tired to go. A large glass of wine before going out used to make me feel alert and less tired.

But once again the con artist was at work in ways that I really could not have imagined and have only understood through my research in the past few years. The bottom line is that alcohol wrecks sleep.

The human body needs between four and six cycles of REM (Rapid Eye Movement) sleep per night, and each cycle last around 90 minutes. Even small amounts of alcohol disrupt sleep, so the REM does not occur, and the sleep we actually get after having a small amount of alcohol equates to between one and two REM cycles.

If you're drinking as I was virtually every night of the week, not only is it seriously damaging your health, but it's also seriously damaging your sleep. The reason I was so tired in the evenings was because I had not had enough replenishing sleep the night before. The sleep I was getting wasn't a refreshing kind of sleep, it was an exhausted kind of sleep. When alcohol starts to withdraw from our system about five hours after our last drink, adrenaline and cortisol floods our body causing our heart to race and the stress response to be triggered. We're ready to fight a war, not get a restful, replenishing night's sleep.

Our sleep is interrupted at the point when our REM sleep naturally deepens, and we don't get enough of it. It has been recently discovered that a lack of REM sleep has an adverse effect on our mental and emotional health. When we enter REM sleep, our subconscious mind processes the unprocessed emotions that we have not expressed during the day.

As adults we have learned not to express every emotion that passes through us during the day. If we howled with tears every time a sad emotion floated through us, or screamed in rage every time something annoyed us, we would be social outcasts. So, we have learned to dampen and control our responses. With alcohol at your side you will be less emotionally capable than you actually are, but without it you will be stronger and your emotional intelligence will soar.

REM sleep allows us to process our emotions, and it is like having our own internal therapy session, and what it means is that we wake up not having a build-up of emotion, and we can start the next day afresh. Without the therapeutic effects of adequate REM sleep we carry an excess of emotions associated with stress into our next day, and we don't cope as well. This, coupled with alcohol-induced anxiety and raised cortisol levels, is not of any benefit to us.

Alcohol is Fun: I Feel Confident and Courageous

As we know, alcohol reduces or even eliminates inhibitions. There is nothing powerful or courageous in being paralytically drunk, smashed, or legless. These words and phrases that are used to describe drunkenness are anything but powerful or courageous. The way that a drug makes you feel is not the way you actually are.

You are courageous when you do something that makes you fearful, and you navigate the fear and do it anyway. You are not courageous when drugs have removed your ability to care, and your ability to function intelligently, and you're making a fool of yourself. You are powerful when you see and hear and react in spite of fear.

You are not powerful when you have these abilities taken away from you. You're not powerful when you don't have the ability to walk in a straight line and people need to shout at you because your ears are no longer hearing properly.

For me, learning to ride a motorbike was one of the most courageous things I've ever done, because at many turns (literally) I found myself terrified! But it was something that I dearly wanted to do, so I ignored my fear and did it anyway.

Everybody knows that Dutch courage is a fake courage. The term refers to the alcohol that was given to the English during the war with the Dutch. Alcohol may have numbed their fear, but it also took away their ability. Sometimes life can feel a bit like a war, but it's better to go into battle with your wits sharply focused and a clear-thinking head.

And when we feel confident enough to speak our alcohol-induced mind? Well, we all know that leads to a world of trouble.

Alcohol is Fun: It Tastes Great

Half a pint of neat alcohol is enough to kill an average person. The taste of ethanol is disgusting. It is processed, diluted and enhanced with flavourings and chemicals to make it palatable. Wine, cider and beer are fermented rotten fruit and vegetables with added chemical flavourings. It is the fruit in wine that gives it its flavour, and it is the juniper or other flavourings in gin that give it its flavour. In recent years, the drinks industry has worked hard to find more tantalising flavourings to add to the ethanol they sell to make it palatable.

This has to be done because no one wants to drink hand sanitiser! If you did, you would vomit, and possibly suffer respiratory failure, go blind, get brain damage, and suffer permanent kidney and liver damage.

Teenagers are encouraged to drink alcohol packaged in brightly coloured bottles with sweet sugary drinks, but it is not the alcohol they like the taste of, it is the sweet sugary drink.

Alcohol in itself tastes disgusting: it is what is added to it for which we have acquired a taste. Even then, a lot of drinks, like wine, beer, vodka, and whiskey were disgusting when we first tasted them, and the reason for this is that our body was trying to reject the poison. This is a natural reaction to poison just like somebody smoking their first cigarette will cough and splutter and gag.

Alcohol is Fun: Sex is Better

While drinking alcohol removes inhibitions, it also reduces ability in the bedroom, and alcohol is the main cause of sexual dysfunction in men, making it harder to become and remain sexually aroused.

And it really is no fun to wake up in the morning with no memory of what happened the night before, and, even worse, not recognising the person next to you in bed! There are significant and real dangers to being drunk and out of control. When drunk, men perceive a greater level of sexual interest from a woman than she intends to communicate. This can lead to unwarranted and unwanted advances, as well as potentially dangerous and threatening situations for women. Alcohol increases a man's sex drive at the same time as reducing his inhibitions, which means that alcohol makes a man vulnerable to his inappropriate behaviour, and a woman vulnerable to the effects of that.

Sex when sober is intimate, loving and present, bringing full awareness and sexual capability to the situation.

Con Stories around Bringing Relief: Alcohol Helps Me!

Alcohol Helps Me: I Feel Less Stressed

Not only has the alcohol con trick convinced us that it adds to our lives in bright, fun and exciting ways, but it also has convinced us that it takes away all the nasties in life. The truth is quite different. We all have difficulties and issues in life, but instead of reducing them or taking them away alcohol increases them.

Over a lifetime a normal drinker is likely to spend around $300,000 on alcohol; for a heavy drinker this could be $500,000, or more. So, for a start, alcohol is taking your money.

The stresses in life are still there to be faced the next morning, only we have now added a horrible hangover, increased tiredness, and drinker's remorse to the problems. Are you better able to deal with life situations when you're feeling well rested, calm, confident and clear headed, or do you think you can better deal with them when you're stressed, feeling sick, and anxious with low self-esteem and worry?

We now know that alcohol causes stress, and it adds to our anxiety.

What this all amounts to is the fact that alcohol never truly relaxes anybody, it just removes the feeling of stress that it caused because we drank alcohol in the first place. It can never relieve stress. Alcohol gives you more and more stress, and makes life harder and harder.

The way to relieve stress and to feel relaxed is to cut off the alcohol supply, and after 7 to 12 days natural calm arrives.

Alcohol Helps Me: It Helps Me After an Argument

Most people will do what they can to avoid confrontation and arguments. Arguments are unpleasant, emotional and sometimes painful. When we are a drinker, we believe that alcohol helps us to deal with negative situations, and so it's understandable that when we feel in pain, angry or wronged, that it would be only natural to reach for a drink to numb the pain.

Drinking after an argument not only numbs the pain, but it also dulls thinking and heightens emotions further. This means that drinking to help with post-argument emotions results in not only making our emotional state worse, but make us more vulnerable to reacting inappropriately, and possibly even putting ourselves in danger.

Alcohol-fuelled arguments and fights are common, because the intelligent, rational part of our brain shuts down. With increased alcohol consumption it's easy to see how the flight response takes over when the fight response has given in, and we become vulnerable to drink driving, having an accident or being out late at night, alone in the dark.

Drinking after an argument doesn't take away any problems, but it does mean that the emotions of the situation are not dealt with properly. Instead, they are still there to welcome you in the morning along with your pounding head, sick stomach and remorseful heart.

No one can ever win an argument or claim the upper hand when they have been consuming alcohol. I regularly had arguments with my partner when we had both been drinking, and we both behaved in ways that we would not have done had we been sober. The result was never pleasant, and it was always very sad, because hurtful things were said about things that would have been overlooked, or not even come to mind, if it hadn't been for alcohol. Hurtful things once said cannot be undone or taken back.

The best way to deal with the outfall of an argument is to take some quiet time for composure and reflection, and to talk things through calmly with a clear head.

As a non-drinker you will have far more confidence to assert yourself and express your feelings and wants and needs. And you will never say something in an alcoholic haze that you will live to regret.

Alcohol Helps Me: It Takes Away My Worries

Worries and concerns are part of everyday life for most people, and coping with worries and concerns both small and large builds an ability and tolerance to cope with further problems. If every problem is faced by reaching into the fridge for the bottle of wine or gin, then no problems are faced at all, and no courage is found to face the next problem.

Over time our 'problem solving' muscles weaken, and our 'alcohol helps everything' muscle gets stronger.

The result is that problems often get worse, and more difficult situations arise caused by alcohol that would never have arisen in the first place.

Worry and anxiety is borne of an emotional response to a specific threat. Healthy concern in the face of genuine threat is important, and is vital to survival, but alcohol always makes any worrisome situation worse because it strips away our natural ability to cope. Alcohol doesn't take away any worries, but it does take away your money, your time, your health, relationships, your self-esteem, and your confidence.

Part 3
Smart People Grow

"Twenty years from now you will be more disappointed by the things you didn't do, than by the ones you did do. So sail away from the safe harbour. Explore. Dream. Discover." Mark Twain

You When You're Smart

BEFORE SHOWING YOU how to walk away from the confidence trickster, and to leave the burning shore to find the shore of calm freedom, let's explore you as the smart person you are without alcohol.

When I discovered that I had been a victim of a long-established con trick it was like I had been sitting in a dark room and someone had turned the lights on. I could see through everything that I had been told and everything that I had experienced, and it was clear to me that the beliefs about alcohol, that I had established over a lifetime, were wrong.

When I understood the truth about alcohol, that it's a highly addictive substance, and when I learned how addiction worked, I could clearly see how the beliefs that I had established were formed. I understand that those beliefs, based on what I knew at the time, were very plausible. This, we now know, is how any con trick works ... it gains your confidence by making you believe what it wants you to believe.

I am sure that many of the things that you now understand about how alcohol gains your confidence, and how alcohol addiction works, have been quite shocking and possibly a revelation to you.

As you have been reading this book you would have been learning facts that were previously unknown to you. All learning is growth, and growth changes us. Once you understand that you have been a victim of a confidence trick, and now that you understand how that confidence trick was played out, you can no longer see it in the same way that you once did.

It's like being shown a magic trick and then having it explained, you can never look at it in the same way that you did before. You will look at it, understand it and experience it from a new sense of awareness and understanding.

The same is true of your understanding and awareness of alcohol. Alcohol was never your friend. There were never any real benefits to taking it, and there are no benefits to taking it now, or ever again. The alcohol con is a clever illusion.

What you believed alcohol was giving you was just a part replacement for what it had already taken away … it was the con artist giving you $10 and then taking $20 when you weren't looking.

For people who are health conscious, just knowing and understanding the appalling health impact of alcohol is enough for them to lose trust, because for them any perceived benefit is outweighed by the potential unknown damage that it is causing.

It is the magnitude of the perceived benefits that has its grip on us, not the real benefits, because there are none.

I have talked a little about human motivations and desires when we looked at the model of motivation that was developed by Maslow. The terminology and the tool itself is not important to remember, but what is important is an understanding of how human beings tick, how we live with hope and aspirations, and how we build our self-esteem and become fulfilled as individuals.

We all have the potential to achieve great things, and to contribute significantly to our families, friends and communities. Alcohol hijacks our natural motivations, aspirations and fulfilment, because once the addiction is established, alcohol settles itself very firmly on the first base of our motivations. It sets itself firmly beside our basic survival needs like food, water and shelter. It is because of this that under certain conditions a drinker will compromise every aspect of their life in pursuit of alcohol and their addiction. They will compromise their family, friends, work and health. They may lose it all with the only thing remaining being alcohol. This is the tragic progression of addiction, and the constant drive to need to fill the void and feel 'normal'. People who remain stuck here remain *floundering*.

But once the confidence trick is understood, the confidence in alcohol is broken, and you will never look at it in the same way again. You don't need to remain *fixated* on alcohol, desperately trying not to drink for your whole life, and labelled with a disease that doesn't exist.

Alcohol has a negative effect on the health of all drinkers, and on the relationships, finance, and work of many. Human beings are not biologically designed to take highly toxic, addictive psychoactive drugs.

If you can achieve all the wonderful things that you have achieved in life with alcohol pulling you down, imagine what you could do without it.

As human beings we all want to do our best, and we want to feel valued, appreciated, and respected. You will have your own values in life that are uniquely true to you, and things that matter to you about who you are. These values underpin everything you are and everything you do.

One of the biggest groups of people becoming addicted to alcohol are people in their 40s, 50s and 60s. Many of these people just like you and I have homes, careers, and families. Many of us have people relying on us who look up to us and model their behaviour on ours.

When we look at our values, what we care about and how we want to be perceived by others, we get a vastly different picture when we throw alcohol into the mix.

Whether it's a family gathering, work event, social outing with friends, or a regular night at home with the kids, alcohol changes you. You now understand about the inebriating effects of alcohol and how it impairs your thinking and alters your behaviour. Think for a moment about some of these behaviour changes and how these relate to your core values.

You may be able to conveniently separate in your own mind the person you are sober from the person you are drunk, but the fact is they are the same person. You are either in alcohol withdrawal the next morning, or you are behaving in all the ways that we associate with a drunk person.

Can you truly say that the person who slurs their words, hurts their loved ones, embarrasses their friends, speaks too honestly to their work colleagues, and falls down drunk, is the person that you want to be?

Nobody is their true selves when they have been drinking, and if you are showing the people that you love the inebriated version of yourself night after night, then you are not only denying yourself those people in your life, you are denying those people the true version of you.

Wine o'clock and half a bottle of wine is enough to change your behaviour and the way you think and talk. One bottle or two bottles of wine and you are no longer yourself. That angry and obnoxious, dopey but not charming, laughing but not funny, and talking but not interesting version of you is not who you are!

If you find yourself getting angry and aggressive when you have been drinking, but not when you haven't been drinking, what does this tell you about the true person you are?

This says that you are not an angry or aggressive person naturally, but that alcohol releases chemicals into your brain and inhibits your normal moderating thoughts. What this tells you is it alcohol warps your thinking and maladapts your emotions, so that when an event happens or something is said, or not said, you will react to it in a way that is entirely as a result of the chemical effects of a drug on your brain.

Do not be fooled into thinking that because alcohol removes inhibitions, the anger or aggression are the true you. You are the true you when you are not drinking, not when you are drinking. Alcohol does remove inhibitions, but it also releases chemicals into your brain and changes your emotional capabilities and your mental capabilities, so you are unable to think, feel and react in the way that you would do without that drug in your system. The drunk angry version of you is drugged. This isn't your inner demons coming out, and it's not the real angry person you are showing their true colors. The angry aggressive drunk is caused by one thing and one thing only: alcohol.

When I was drinking, my loved ones were unhappy with the person I was when I had been drinking. Given what we now know about alcohol, there is little surprise in that. I said hurtful things and I behaved in hurtful ways. Alcohol made me angry, depressed, emotional, and sometimes aggressive. When I was a drinker I thought that this was my true nature coming out with a drink. I thought that I was able to control myself during the day, but with my inhibitions released the true me came out.

It saddens me deeply to realise today that the person I was when I was sober was the true me, the go-getting, life-loving, calm, kind, considerate and compassionate person that I fully know I am today.

Is any of this worth it just so that we, along with every other drinker on the planet, can convince ourselves that with a drink in our hand we can become the life and soul of the party?

Does it even really matter if there is a life and soul of the party? Do you really want to go to a party knowing that half the time you are going to get beaten up on the way home? Because you now see that those are probably the best odds you have got, and alcohol is likely to beat you up by the next morning.

When we were children, we were able to have fun and laugh and play without the need for drugs, and we still have that ability. When we take away the con artist, and unleash it from our lives, life becomes simpler, more fulfilling, and more rewarding. As a non-drinker you will find that you are completely true to the essence of who you are, and to your values, all the time, and you will not have the destructive force of alcohol proving otherwise.

The Morning After Con

DRINKER'S REMORSE IS a real thing. It's that sinking feeling when you come to consciousness the day after the night before, and the creeping nausea sets in the pit of your stomach, as you remember (or try to remember) what you did and said the night before.

Did your children see you drunk on the sofa? Did you fall and hurt yourself? Did you say or do something hurtful, or worse still, did you cause hurt or pain to someone else? Did you put yourself at risk?

I understand well those feelings, because I woke up with them periodically for 20 years.

What I didn't know or understand was that millions of other people were waking up feeling the same way. I thought there was something wrong with me, and I thought that the problem was uniquely mine.

People are open to talk about how they can't wait to get back home for wine o'clock or can't wait to meet their mates in the pub for the 6pm gin and tonic, but no one ever talks about how they wake up with guilt, shame and dread.

That's the dark, dirty secret that we all keep to ourselves. The con artist wants to keep us silent.

So, what is drinker's remorse? For a start, it's the genuine concern about what happened the night before, and the automatic feeling of guilt and shame. But it is also the withdrawal effects of alcohol, which can be considerable, as anxiety and stress hormones course through your body. Add to this dehydration, toxins, and nausea, and you are left feeling all round dreadful. So, on top of waking up and remembering or trying to remember the bad behaviour from the night before, we also suffer heightened levels of anxiety because of the withdrawal effects of alcohol itself.

None of these feelings are good for a person's self-esteem or wellbeing, and yet we continue to drink regardless of these effects, for as long as we're still being fooled and are still being played in the alcohol con.

As you now know, alcohol, the alcohol industry and everything you have ever you thought you knew and trusted about alcohol is a lie.

The lake is an illusion, there are no fire-breathing dragons or monsters, and the lake is a mirage just like a road surface on a hot day.

All that is needed is to walk away from the confidence trickster and never look back.

The alcohol con artist is clever in many ways. When it grips and we're floundering on the hook trying to gain control, you now know that just like the fish, the victim of a con artist becomes a victim the minute the con artist makes contact. The second the fish believed that the lure was real, it was already trapped.

Smart Recap

WE HAVE LEARNT MANY important facts about how the alcohol con works. All of the points below are covered in the book, and if you are not convinced by any of them, please go back to the relevant section. Here is your recap:

- Alcohol is a highly addictive drug, and consuming a highly addictive drug leads to addiction.

- Every drink of alcohol fills the void caused by the last drink, giving rise to the belief that alcohol provides a benefit when it is only partially relieving the void that it created.

- Every drink of alcohol releases stress hormones into the body. Over time, a tolerance is built to the poison, and the body needs more alcohol to achieve less relief than it did previously.

- Willpower and forced behaviour change is ineffective as a method of controlling alcohol, because it starts a battle of wills in your head between your conscious mind and your subconscious mind.

- Someone who is addicted to alcohol is not weak and has nothing wrong with them.

They have fallen for the alcohol con along with millions of other intelligent people.

- The subconscious mind is like a child: sometimes helpful and sometimes troublesome. This child has been fooled by the alcohol con artist to believe that it is helping when it tells you to have a drink when you feel stressed, or bored, or anxious, or reckless, or happy, or excited.

- The only thing that alcohol does is fool you, while it takes more from you and gives nothing in return.

- When we want to stop drinking, we believe that it will be painful to stop, and that alcohol will be impossible to live without. This belief is based on the seeing others who have tried to stop drinking and failed, seeing others who have stopped drinking and live every day in sufferance, and any beliefs we haven't yet worked through that alcohol is beneficial.

- There are no true benefits to alcohol whatsoever.

Stopping drinking alcohol is easy now you know the truth and have seen through the con.

Stepping Free

YOU HAVE LEARNT SO much about the alcohol con and the reasons why it has worked in the way it has up until now. You may already know that you never want to drink again, and you may have already embraced the wonderful freedom of sobriety.

The burning shore where resources are running out is a mirage, and it is the path of alcohol addiction. The opposite shore is but one small step away and that small step will release you immediately and permanently from the grips of the con artist.

You have been experiencing the physical symptoms of withdrawal for as long as you have been drinking, and you've been experiencing the physical symptoms of withdrawal at the current level that you are now for years.

It takes between seven and twelve days for alcohol to completely be removed from your system and all the toxins and poisons with it.

For a few days you may feel a little anxious or agitated as your body realises that it doesn't need to pump out so much cortisol and adrenaline to counteract the depressive effects of the alcohol. Be kind, it will pass.

In the past, the reason that your desire to drink was so strong was because when your subconscious mind told you to drink you trusted it, and you listened to it. You now know your subconscious mind is like a child, and it tries to help you and protect you. But it has not been helpful or protective because it has been fooled, just like you may have once believed in Father Christmas and harmless fairy tales. Your child-like subconscious has been a victim of the alcohol con, and over months and years it has misled you, even though it had the best intentions.

The abuser and the hustler in this con was alcohol and you were the victim. Freedom is more than just rejoicing, freedom is about leaving you triumphant as you step out into the world victorious, newly aware, acutely conscious that you are now more than capable of outsmarting the con artist.

You don't need to flounder, or remain fixated, caught in the trap of trying to change your behaviour without first changing your thinking.

We have now completed the process laid out at the beginning of Part 2, in Let's Get Smart. If there is anything from that process that is still keeping you stuck it is just because a concept hasn't quite clicked yet, that is all. You can go back to the relevant sections now and re-read them.

If everything so far has made sense to you, then to completely break free, you must do five things:

> 1. Believe in your power to take control of your child-like subconscious mind now that it has been re-educated.

2. Feel excited in the knowledge that you are walking to freedom, capable and confident.

3. Over the course of the next two weeks you must rejoice every time every slight nagging feeling of alcohol withdraws from your system because you now know that it is leaving forever. It's just the security guard trying to do their job. Be kind, but firm.

4. Allow yourself permission to think about alcohol should the thought come into your head. Allow those thoughts to float by and, as you do, thank your subconscious mind for trying to be helpful and then ignore its advice because you now know better, and you have no desire to entertain the con artist any longer.

5. Always be grateful and never complacent about your decision to outsmart the con artist and get out of the trap.

Just One Drink Now and Then

IF YOU'RE STILL UNSURE about your ability or desire to never drink again ask yourself why you would ever want to entertain the con artist again. But if you think you can live harmoniously with it, let it be clear why you can't.

We started drinking as a young person with no intention of ending up at the point where we were stuck in a trap and where with every drink of alcohol we fell further. This is the nature of alcohol, and it cannot be changed. We fell because of the drug and how it hijacks our natural biology, and not because of our nature or inability to control our use of a drug.

One drink of alcohol is all that it takes to re-establish the void which will then be crying out to be filled by another drink.

A word of warning. Over time, the mind has an amazing capacity to forget the bad things that have happened. Psychologically this process is called 'fading affect bias'. Essentially, fading affect bias means that the negative aspect of any event or situation fades away in our memory more quickly than the positive ones.

This is believed to be so that we live our lives more positively and with hope, despite negative experiences. This represents a potential threat to a person enjoying newfound sobriety, because it means that the reasons that prompted you to stop drinking will fade quicker than the dopamine-soaked party memories.

As a non-drinker you may forget how you felt mentally and emotionally when you woke up in a cold sweat with a pounding heart, nausea, shame and dread. You may forget the look in the eyes of your children or loved ones the day after they had suffered from your drunken ramblings, foolishness, or abuse, and you may forget the fear of the health implications.

At this point you will be vulnerable once more to the effects of the con artist, so be prepared. Knowledge is power, and, now that you are aware of fading affect bias and the way it may affect your thinking, you are in a position where you can be prepared and respond positively. Many people keep a short summary of exactly what their life was like when they were caught in the con. This can serve as a timely reminder if fading affect bias means that you find the negative aspects of being conned become less pronounced in your mind.

One drink was all that was needed for you as a young drinker to become addicted to alcohol and to have an alcohol problem. Nothing has changed, apart from the fact that you now understand that you were a victim of a long, protracted, and painful confidence trick. One drink will put you back in its clutches.

There are other ways in which the con artist may try to worm his way back into your trust.

Curiosity

AFTER A YEAR OF COMPLETELY enjoying sobriety I stumbled into the clutches of the con artist once more in what, at the time, was the most surprising circumstance. I'm here to warn you about curiosity so that you can guard yourself against it.

There is a constant and continuous bombardment on us all from many angles of our lives, where alcohol will try, as it did many years ago, to win our confidence and pique our interest. After a year of being sober I became curious. I had no desire whatsoever for alcohol, but I am a scientist and I was curious, and I wondered what it would be like to sit around the table with everybody else and have a drink of alcohol. I was curious as to whether I would like the taste, and I was curious about how it would make me feel, if indeed anything at all. Everyone else was doing it, and like the child growing up in a society of drinkers I was simply curious.

So, I had a drink. It didn't taste very nice and it didn't have any effect on me. I didn't feel any different. So, my curiosity didn't go away, and it remained. I was still curious because the glass of wine tasted horrible and had no effect on me. So, the next time there was wine on the table I had a drink, only this time I had two glasses. Those two drinks seemed to have little effect on me either. So, I continued with my curiosity and I decided to turn it into an experiment: my alcohol experiment.

Two months after my initial curiosity was piqued, I first suggested to my work colleague that we pop to the pub for a drink after work. Two days later I suggested we did the same again. By now I was having a gin and tonic when I was preparing the dinner in the evening. I thought that gin wasn't the same as wine so I'd be okay, and it wouldn't cause a problem. A couple of weeks later I found myself getting a bit touchy on the way home from work, and I found myself feeling a horrible low-level discomfort similar to hunger. I felt on edge and it made me feel agitated. That word 'agitated' describes how I felt exactly, as though I couldn't settle. When I got home to my family, I remained agitated. And the agitation went away after I'd poured myself a gin and tonic.

That was where my experiment ended. My curiosity and my experiment were both satisfied that I was missing out on absolutely nothing. But I had forgotten to include one very important factor in my journey: I had stopped being grateful, and after a year of freedom I had taken my sobriety for granted and I had looked over at the con artist wondering what it would be like if I played around the edges, and wondering if it would be different this time.

That is why I added the fifth point in the list of instructions.

Gratitude is a huge reminder of what we have in our lives, our place in time and space and the people we share it with. As you read through the last few paragraphs you would have seen that I went through the same stages in the con trick once again, only this time what took me from 10 to 30 years the first time round happened over the course of two months.

Be aware of curiosity, and if and when it arises remember the curiosity that the young drinker once had, and be grateful for your sobriety. The curiosity of the young drinker was understandable, and you were already a mark for the con artist from the minute you were born. Know that your curiosity was satisfied once, and let it be satisfied for good.

Be courageous and be bold. There is a world of curiosity to be satisfied in your life. Adventures to be had, peace to find, and a life to thrive at with crisp clarity. Don't waste your curiosity looking down the neck of a bottle of wine.

Thinking about Drinking

WITH SO MANY INFLUENCES from alcohol in all walks of society it is completely unrealistic and unnecessary to try to stop thinking about alcohol.

It is completely expected and normal for you to think about alcohol, and especially true for that to be the case in the early days of your sobriety. When those thoughts of alcohol come to your mind remember to be grateful that you are finally free, and to be triumphant that you've outsmarted the biggest con trick of our time.

Let those thoughts come and let them go. If your helpful and well-meaning subconscious mind interprets any of those thoughts by suggesting that they mean you want to drink, simply tell it otherwise and thank it for its consideration. You're the boss, you now know better and your subconscious mind is learning that. You have strength, courage and most importantly, knowledge on your side. The wrong knowledge educated your subconscious and conscious minds previously, and it is the correct knowledge that has now re-educated the way you think and given you the power to outsmart the con.

Be confident in your thoughts when alcohol passes through your awareness, and when you see images of alcohol dressed up in the media. When you see people drinking alcohol and you hear their comments, remind yourself that they are still caught up in the alcohol con and that you have expertise and knowledge that they don't yet have.

From time to time events will trigger your subconscious mind to think that alcohol is a solution. There is no need to worry when this happens. Remember that the administrator only has old records at hand to give you advice, and the old records are no longer helpful to you. Alcohol memories are soaked in dopamine and are not real. Smile and ignore them. Just remind yourself of this, be happy to be free, and go ahead and take a new path, writing a new record for your mental library to access next time.

Replacements

WHEN YOU FIRST STOP drinking alcohol you may wonder about replacing the time you spent drinking with time doing something equally mundane. There is no point replacing one addiction in your life for another. People often find that when they stop drinking alcohol a sweet tooth that they never had suddenly appears and they find themselves with a craving for sugar. Drinking alcohol was something you did when you were addicted to alcohol. There is no need to try to replace it with a quick sugar high.

Non-alcoholic versions of alcoholic drinks are a strange phenomenon and one to be aware of because anything that is designed to impersonate a drug will send a message to the subconscious that there is some value in the drug in the first place.

Wine is made from fermented fruit, whereas non-alcoholic wine isn't. It's not wine at all. It is fruit juice cleverly packaged by brand managers and advertising agencies to fool people who wish that it did have alcohol in it and to make them acutely conscious that they may be missing out. Non-alcoholic versions of alcoholic drinks are for drinkers to make themselves feel a little less like they're missing out on something. Something that we now know is causing them no benefit whatsoever.

If you're unsure about the flawed logic of replacement just think for a moment about how vaping has become a common verb in our language. Where people used to smoke, they now vape. You may argue that non-alcoholic drinks don't contain alcohol, whereas e-cigarettes do contain nicotine. The point is that non-alcoholic drinks are designed to be substitutes and something that substitutes something else is replacing it. An addiction is something to remove, the alcohol con is something to end, and the trap is something to get out of. It would be crazy, wouldn't it, to find something to replace a trap?

Far better to walk away with a smile. Sure, you will need and want something refreshing and good tasting to drink, but with the growing rise in the sober revolution there are many delicious tasting drinks that stand on their own two feet because of that. These drinks are refreshing, taste great, and aren't pretending to be something they're not.

Our brains have something called 'neuroplasticity', which essentially means that they are malleable and capable of change. New neural pathways form and old pathways wither.

The process of breaking free and staying free from alcohol is a process of forming new neural pathways in your brain, and them firing and wiring together to form strong and established pathways that thoughts shoot down when triggered.

Imagine a meadow with long grass. When you first walk through the grass, the next day it will probably not be noticeable that you were there, so the next day if you follow the same path you will again be walking through long grass. After a couple of days a new path begins to form, and this will widen and become more marked and clear with time. If you enjoy walking down the path and are happy to be there, and filled with gratitude, it will become a go-to place for you.

This is the analogy of your new path in life without alcohol, and after a while the old alcohol-response pathway will grow over.

Do everything you can to strengthen the pathway. At wine o'clock take the opportunity to build another new connection: feel proud and excited about your future, smile at how smart you are for outsmarting the con artist, do something soothing, enjoyable and positive. It doesn't need to be much to strengthen the new pathway, and it doesn't need to be a chore. Just feeling great about your decision and being free is enough.

Part 4
Adjusting to a Life of Freedom

"Freedom is a journey of discovery that brings a smile to your lips, pride to your heart, and a spring in your step"
Michaela Weaver

When Life is More

AS A CONFIDENT NON-drinker you will have more money, you will enjoy better health, you will be calmer than you could have imagined, and you will be more capable and able to deal with the challenges in life.

You will be able to go out in the evenings without ever having to worry about how you're getting home. You will remember every moment of your life in crystal clear fashion.

When I stopped drinking, I saved so much money in the first year that I treated myself to a motorbike licence and a motorbike, something that I always wanted but never thought I would be able to do. My new hobby has introduced me to wonderful people who have now become lifelong friends. Together we enjoy adventures and social evenings, and I have travelled with my partner across Europe on my 1000cc motorbike.

This is my first non-fiction book, and I have decided that I am going to dedicate the rest of my career to helping people who want to outsmart the con artist and live their lives free from alcohol. I made this decision when my father was diagnosed with cancer. It shocked and shook my world, and three weeks after the diagnosis, I quit my day job, and decided that I had to help to make a difference to the lives of people ensnarled in addiction. This book is dedicated to him, his courage, and lifelong inspiration and support.

There are things waiting for you in your future without alcohol that you will not even be able to imagine. There are real relationships that don't revolve around alcohol, and the relationships you have will be so much stronger.

The relationship that will outshine all others in your life of sobriety will be the relationship you have with yourself. You will walk through your life as a conscious and competent non-drinker, fully aware of the con trick that you have outsmarted, and freed yourself from. You will live a life that is bright and vivid in colour and experience.

With alcohol out of your life you can begin to focus wholeheartedly on the motivations that drive you to live a fulfilled and fulfilling life. Alcohol will no longer be fighting and vying for position in your survival needs, because your survival needs will be met through the food and drinks that nourish you.

Your security needs will be met through the work that you are able to apply yourself to, and the home that you are able to provide. In times of difficulty when your survival or security needs may be challenged you can now be confident that you are managing those from a position of power, where you can bring the best of everything that is you to those situations with full consciousness and capability.

You will not be facing any future challenges with an internal war battling inside your head between your subconscious and your conscious minds.

You will not be facing life and its challenges in a constant state of withdrawal from a drug because you will not be living in a state of addiction. Even as you approach life's challenges you will still have a freedom that you can wake up every day being proud of and grateful for.

The freedom that you have earned yourself will help you to fulfil greater motivations beyond survival and security. I hope that you go on to fulfil the potential of your life and thrive in every possible aspect, and that you contribute to society in a way that brings you wellbeing and joy. Your life of sobriety will be one lived where the values that matter to you and the person that you want to be are in complete alignment.

Many of the people who fall victim to the alcohol con trick are those that most break the stereotypical view of 'an alcoholic'. There are millions of people living with alcohol addiction who are well-educated university and college graduates. These people are often leaders in our society. The alcohol con does not care who you are, and well-educated successful people are more likely to have the social networks and the financial means to give the alcohol addiction a good run for its money. Lawyers, doctors, politicians, accountants, nurses, teachers, engineers and scientists, dentists, entrepreneurs and intrapreneurs are all as likely to fall into the alcohol trap as anybody else.

Outsmarting alcohol is about exposing the con and encouraging you to learn about alcohol and addiction long before you lose everything that you value, and your life falls apart. But even if you have hit the rock at the bottom there is still hope, and there is still time to get out.

A Life of Calm

EXPLAINING THE CALM that comes after the storm of alcohol addiction is difficult, because it is only through experiencing it that you will truly feel the difference in your life.

There will be worries and concerns in life, but you will be approaching them from a position of calm rather than from a position of agitation. This gives you a buffer zone, in which many of the small worries in life will be accommodated, and you won't have the same feelings of stress and agitation in the face of them that you would have had before.

A completely unexpected pleasure of removing the wine o'clock hours and weekend binges from my life was my wonderful crystal-clear mornings. I told you previously that when I was drinking, I generally thought that I was an evening person, but I was a drunk evening person and a hungover morning person most of the time. I now wake up and am alert straight away in the mornings, and practice yoga or run to the beach or spend a precious morning hour doing other things that add value to my life. I love my mornings, and I am confident that you will too.

When you walk away from the con artist you will benefit in other ways too. You will have better sleep, more energy, clarity of thinking, clearer skin, more hydration in your body, increased mental focus, better digestion, increased absorption of vitamins and minerals, weight loss due to less caloric intake, reduced risk of heart disease or breast cancer, a better immune system, and improved memory function. That's a lot of benefits!

Being Smart on A Drunk Planet

YOU MAY FIND IT STRANGE when you first walk out into the world with your new knowledge and freedom when everyone around you is still drinking. I remember walking into a bar and looking at everybody pouring poison down their throats and it felt horrifying. I wanted to scream at them to stop, but of course I didn't. The fact is that now you're smart about alcohol, and the rest of the planet is way behind you. Most people you know will either be stuck at the point of being frozen and unconscious of what they are doing, or they will be floundering, caught on the hook of addiction, but unable to get off.

When you're smart on a drunk planet here's what you need to know.

- Avoid telling other people anything that you've learned unless they specifically ask for your help or advice.

- Never tell a friend or partner that they have a problem, unless the risk of not telling them is greater than them picking a fight with you. They will be in denial, and they will respond like a cornered animal. The best way to approach this is to lead by example.

- You do have a super-power, so enjoy it. You outsmarted the con artist that is fooling

191

everyone who has alcohol in their glass. Be smug, just do it subtly.

- Never feel that you are missing out, because you will always feel better than a drinker who is drinking to fill the void caused by their last drink.

Social Situations

THE SITUATIONS THAT often cause people most concern when they are considering stopping drinking alcohol are the social occasions in life, such as parties, weddings, holidays, after-work drinks, and meeting friends in a bar. Alcohol, after all, is the only drug that you have to justify not taking.

When I stopped drinking alcohol, I had different reactions from different people. There were the people who rudely and loudly laughed away my sobriety, those who shuffled their feet not knowing where to look, and those who poured themselves an extra-large glass of wine. All of those people were themselves caught in the alcohol trap and were struggling with denial. When you experience these reactions yourself, you will know what is underpinning them.

Then there were people full of admiration, like I was some superwoman blessed with strange and mystic powers. These people were baffled because they could not imagine ever being able to live without wine in their lives. They too were caught up in the con.

Then there were people who found me at a quiet moment and asked me if I thought they had a problem with alcohol, and who were worried. They too were caught up in the con.

Everyone who drinks alcohol on any regular basis is caught. Some people know it, and some people are still frozen in a state of unknowing, but alcohol is addictive, and people get addicted to addictive substances.

Social situations often cause people some anxiety. This is normal, and even beneficial, because we're a social species and we want to be liked and to fit in. One way to guarantee not to be sociable and likeable is to get blind drunk, insult everybody and fall over. At the time, in your drug-induced state, you may feel like you're the most hilarious person on the planet, but you're not. You're being an arse and embarrassing yourself.

In the social situations you will find yourself in, many of the drinkers will be envious of you, because you have walked away from a con that they suspect that they too have fallen for, but they don't think they can leave.

You will find that you are quietly admired by people, and you can certainly feel proud of yourself.

When you socialise sober you are fully conscious of what you are saying and doing. You are an interested and compassionate listener, rather than an over-zealous, gabbling talker. Being truly present and interested in people and your surroundings is a gift. You don't need to be drugged to be with other human beings and have a good time.

Just watch drinkers around you relax when they get a glass in their hands, and remember that you don't feel their level of stress or urgency to get the drug in your hands. Drinkers drink to feel normal, but never get there, whereas you are always in that place. Enjoy it.

After a couple of drinks, the alcohol starts to shut down parts of the drinkers' brains, and after a couple more they start to slur, repeat themselves and get sensitive and argumentative.

If you are at a boring party or social event, then as a non-drinker you may quite rightly feel bored, but if it's a great event, or a bar with a lovely atmosphere, then finding yourself in a crowd full of people who are inebriated is liberating. So do what you want, because the only person who will remember with crystal clarity is you! Let your hair down and dance like no one will remember watching you. If you want to, be frivolous and carefree.

Without alcohol, everything that you do when you're out socially is a conscious decision, and you know that you can stand by it the next day. It's an unfortunate truth that the same cannot be said of the people in the corner of the bar downing vodka and tonics.

If, after celebrating your escape from the con, you continue to find social events awkward for a while then the best way to resolve this is to practice kindness and compassion to yourself. If you have spent many years having a swift glass or two of wine before attending a social event to help you overcome social anxiety, then your coping mechanisms will take some time to strengthen because you've not needed them before. You'll soon adapt and will be stronger for it.

Be kind to yourself and take baby steps. Spend some time at these events just quietly observing what you see around you, relax and listen. Remember that when you were a drinker you may have thought you were the life and soul of the party, and that is exactly what the drinkers around you think they are now. Just watch the life and souls of the party getting slowly more drunk, as you sit there becoming more self-assured. Every time you go into a social event as a non-drinker your confidence and your capabilities will be growing, as you learn perhaps for the first time to navigate these situations without alcohol. Most drinkers will be far too worried about getting their own glass topped up to worry about what's in yours.

The Final Fears of Saying Goodbye

AS HUMANS WE ALL HAVE a propensity to fear change, and yet we know that change is a constant in our lives. Everything that we have ever done and achieved had to be done from a point of unknowing. And yet we did, and we achieved.

This means that you know with absolute certainty that you are highly capable of doing things today that you have not done before. It doesn't matter particularly whether there is anxiety or uncertainty attached to doing something, what matters is that you do it.

There is one certain way to fail at doing something and that is to not do it at all. You have the choice to stay on the burning shore, and live in the grip of the con artist, or you can step out tentatively and do something you've never done before.

You may argue that you have given up alcohol before. This time you know that you are not giving up anything. You are saying goodbye to the most toxic and poisonous psychological relationship that you've ever had. All you need to do is be quietly assertive when the subconscious child tries to help you by suggesting that the best thing to do is to have a drink. When you say goodbye to the con artist, you'll be reminding that child calmly and confidently that isn't what you do any more.

You're about to do something amazing and it will be amongst the best, if not the best thing that you have ever done. You may not know it yet. But you soon will.

Here are some stories from others before you...

Thank you so much! The insight you have shared has changed my life! I have a new-found confidence and been able to leave behind the guilt I felt with alcohol.

I am currently working on certification to empower women and young girls through coaching. This is something that I have considered for a few years now.

Being sober has given me the extra confidence to go forward with my dream, without feeling like I'm living a double life.

I know that reaching out and "paying it forward" is the most rewarding thing in life that I can do!

Thank you so much! I'm so thankful that you are willing to share your story to help others.

Lisa

Hi Michaela

Wow, I haven't had a drink for weeks and feel really proud of myself.

Gradually losing some weight and now able to follow a sensible eating plan to lose more.

Thanks for introducing me to these concepts. I'm feeling very grateful to you for enabling me to take control.

Cheers, Penny

Hi Michaela, Thank you so much. Your program has been the best thing ever for me. Changing my thoughts with your techniques has been amazing. 5 weeks and no alcohol. Don't even miss it. I feel free, happy and in control of my life for the first time ever. I have suffered anxiety since I was a child and have used alcohol as a coping tool since I was very young. I am almost 60 and now realise how the alcohol has only enhanced my anxiety all these years. I am now virtually anxiety free. I have never!!! felt this good. A million thank you's!!!!!!! Andrea

Hi Michaela. I drank at home alone for so many years while functioning with the rest of my life outwardly. Inwardly I was sinking lower until I came across you. I haven't had alcohol for over 13 months and have no desire for it either! Thank you. Trish

Hi Michaela. Thank you so much for guiding me through the journey to being sober. Reflecting on my life to date I have used alcohol as a crutch since being a shy teenager through all the challenges and uncertainties of university, professional and family life and, most recently through the increased anxiety during menopause. I had become addicted and was in a bottle-of-wine-a-night habit. The determination and will power I used in life to achieve academic success, eat well and train hard for triathlons just didn't work when I wanted to stop drinking. Your clear explanation of the addiction cycle made so much sense and gave me the key to escape the alcohol trap. I am discovering the joys of relaxation, exercise and clear-headed early mornings and looking forward with great anticipation to my sober life. You have changed my life and I thank you. Judy

I'm seven months alcohol free today so just thought I'd share. I'm pleased with my progress and truly believe if I can do it anyone can. So, be proud of your successes and be kind to yourself if a hiccup occurs. That's all it needs to be 'just a hiccup'. Thanks again Michaela. You and your programme have help me change my life. Wendy

I was a lifelong drinker and the quantity of my wine consumption increased along with my career success. I knew my health, physical and mental, was suffering but every day I said no more and wine o clock would come around and I was helpless. I always managed dry January, Sober October but I knew I was much less in control of the wine than the wine being in control of me. That was until I discovered Michaela's programme. The programme was science based and helped me rewire my brain to banish those rose-tinted memories associated with wine. Every single module made sense to me, and it was delivered compassionately which helped me be less hard on myself. I learned that my increased drinking was not my fault! From day one on the programme I had hope that I'd become alcohol free, and I have. I have absolutely no desire for alcohol and my house is still full of it. Michaela's approach works. Participate fully, do the homework and, if you're like me, there will be no going back. Freedom from alcohol is life-changing and I am grateful daily to Michaela for her fantastic programme. Alison

Join Us

IF YOU HAVE FOUND THIS book beneficial, please tell a friend who may still be frozen in the alcohol con.

For further support and advice on breaking free and staying free you will find information on my website www.thealcoholcoach.com

You can also find inspiration and link with me on social media:

https://www.facebook.com/TheAlcoholCoach/

https://www.instagram.com/thealcoholcoach/

Made in the USA
Las Vegas, NV
22 April 2021